ALL OF
TURKEY

205 Colour illustrations

NET

INDEX

Credits:

Photo from the Archives of Casa Editrice Bonechi taken by Luigi Di Giovine, Paolo Giambone e Andrea Pistolesi.
Photo NET: pages 3, 5, 6, 12, 24, 28-31, 33-44, 61 above, 64-68, 70, 72-78, 91-96, 98 above, 99, 100, 106-108, 145-157.
Photo Gaetano Barone: pages 69, 71, 90, 97, 98 below.
Photo Nicola Grifoni: pages 4, 32.

ISBN 88-7009-271-2

* * *

The church of Hagia Sophia, in Istanbul,
seen from above.

INTRODUCTION

Geographically Turkey is a sort of gravitational center between the West and the East, a point of junction between continental and peninsular Europe and the immense mass of the Afro-Asian continent. From the dawn of civilization this age-old land has been a sort of symptomatic indicator in the complex delicate mechanism of the precarious states of equilibrium which existed on the shores of the Mediterranean.
Tourist literature often uses the terms "land of contrasts" and "Gate to the Orient" when speaking of Turkey, and while these phrases have a measure of truth to them, they are little compared with what the modern state of Turkey really is — an immense container of art, history and culture. Stretching out towards the Mediterranean in the direction of the con-

tinental mass of Europe from which it is separated by the Bosphorus and the Dardanelles, modern-day Turkey offers the tourist the picturesqueness of its enchanted shores, the spell and seduction of Istanbul *(ancient* Constantinople*), treasures of art and nature in* Cappadocia, *the marvels of* Pamukkale, *the mystery of* Nemrud Dağ *and the boundless silences of* Mount Ararat.
What once went by the name of Asia Minor *offers an inexhaustible variety of things to see in the fields of art and architecture, ranging from the remains of the ancient Hittite and Urartean civilizations, to the archaeological ruins of the Hellenistic period, the remains of the Roman past, the manifest vestiges of the Christian-Byzantine age, and the manifestations of Seljuk and*

3

Ottoman art. Along the Aegean and Mediterranean shores and in the neighboring hinterland archaeological sites abound and it is hard to choose between them. The enigmatic ruins of Homer's Troy, the Hellenistic splendor of Pergamum, the marvelous vestiges of Ephesus, and the spectacular allure of Aphrodisias are only the most evident and striking notes in an archaeological context one cannot help but marvel at and admire.

This incredible patrimony of art and culture is the stratification of historical events whose roots lie hidden in the mists of time. Inhabited since earliest times, Anatolia witnessed the passage of power from one civilization to another: the Hittites (18th-13th cent. B.C.), the Phrygians, the Lydians. While the Greek colonies were establishing their first settlements on the Aegean coast, the Persians were gaining control of the entire region (6th-5th cent. B.C.) . In the second half of the 4th century B.C. Alexander the Great's expedition was a prelude to the advent of the Hellenistic kingdoms which were later assimilated by the Roman empire (1st cent. A.D.). From 324 A.D. on, with the elevation of Constantinople to the rank of imperial capital, what is now Istanbul lived one of its periods of greatest splendor. The Byzantine empire gave way to the Seljuk Turks who were in turn replaced by the Ottoman Turks (15th cent.) until their vast empire disintegrated (18th-19th cent.). After a long period of conflicts on a European scale, during which the country was also occupied by foreign powers, the proclamation of the Republic (Oct. 29, 1923), thanks to Atatürk, marked the real beginnings of modern Turkey.

A characteristic sight in the Turkish landscape: the ruins of a caravanserai in the midst of the verdant plain.

The mosque of Sultan Selim (Selimiye Camii), in Edirne, is the architect Sinan's masterpiece.

EDIRNE

The city, known also as *Hadrianopolis*, is the second largest city of so-called "European Turkey". Its felicitous geographical site, practically on the Greek border and extremely close to the Bulgarian frontier, makes it a real "gateway" to Turkey for tourists from Europe. It is one of the principal cities in the province of Thrace and a major center for trade and commerce, as well as active culturally and with an important military garrison.

First ascertained historical documents refer to a town inhabited by peoples from Thrace. The foundation of Hadrianopolis dates to the first half of the 2nd century A.D. and the name itself preserves the memory of the Roman emperor Hadrian. Fortified by Theodosius with a new circuit of walls, it was a sort of outpost for nearby Constantinople. A flourishing Venetian port of call (11th cent.), its vicissitudes were many and it ended up under Turkish dominion in the 14th century, becoming the seat of Osman supremacy. In recent times the functions of the city have centered on its role as

military and strategic strongpoint; the so-called Peace of Hadrianopolis (Sept. 14, 1829) ratified the end of the conflict between Russia and Turkey.

The most popular tourist attraction is the mosque known as **Selimiye Camii**, built in the second half of the 16th century by the architect Sinan, using elements of Egyptian, Greek and Byzantine provenance. Fully 999 windows open in the fabric of the building which has a vast dome supported by mighty pillars, while four slender minarets frame the entire complex. Of particular note are the fine majolica decorations on the *mihrab*.

The **Eski Camii** or *Old Mosque* (15th cent.) represents the oldest example of Ottoman architecture in Hadrianopolis. Close by, note should be taken of the covered market (*bedestan*), distinguished by the number of domes that rise up from the roof, and the *Caravanserai of Rüstem Paşa*, recently restored on the basis of the original project.

The so-calle **Mosque of the Three Galleries** was built

A monument in one of the city squares has been dedicated to the wrestlers who, with well-oiled bodies, exhibit themselves in public matches.

in the first half of the 15th century by the Ottoman Sultan Murad II, who was a major patron of buildings in Hadrianopolis. From an architectural point of view the structure, topped by four minarets, is highly interesting. Nearby are the 15th-century Turkish Baths (*Sokurlu Hamam*), still used, and the rather sorry remains of two *madrasas*.

One of Murad II's buildings particularly worthy of note is the charming **Muradiye**, striking for its smaller scale and fine majolica decor, that was slightly earlier. Formerly it was the seat of the religious sect of the *Whirling Dervishes*.

Lastly mention must be made of the **Bayazit Camii** (15th cent.), a complex of buildings with Koran schools, a hostel for the needy, a pharmacy and kitchens, of a few old bridges in the city, and a tower, all that is left of the fortifications erected by Hadrian to defend the city.

Panorama of the city.

ISTANBUL

In 658 B.C. a group of Dorian colonists under King Byzas founded a colony on the European shores of the Bosphorus, in a tranquil sheltered port. Thanks to this felicitous geographical position (through the straits of the Bosphorus the Black Sea communicates with the Sea of Marmara which in turn via the Dardanelles empties out into the Mediterranean) Byzantium soon became an important trading center, attracting the attention of Darius of Persia, who conquered it in 513 B.C. Subsequently the city made a pact of alliance with Rome, and while the latter, worn out by the continuous Barbarian invasions, was on the wane, the star of Byzantium was growing ever brighter. In 324 A.D. Constantine reunited the two parts of the Empire and on May 11, 330, he solemnly consecrated the city as the new capital with the name of Nea Roma, or New Rome. It was however better known as Constantinople and the Byzantine civilization that was created here shone for centuries. Constantinople reached the heights of its splendor under the Emperor Justinian, sole head of Church and State.

At the end of the 11th century, the spiritual tensions that characterized the West, together with the idea of liberating the holy places of Jerusalem from the Infidels, led to the Crusades. In April of 1204 the Christian knights conquered Constantinople, where they plundered and killed without pity, pillaged and destroyed. Countless art treasures of inestimable value were lost. With no more than a hundred thousand inhabitants, its past splendor gone, the city was reconquered by the Byzantine Empire just as the Ottoman Turks were beginning their inexorable march. In 1451 the able and ambitious Sultan Mohammed II rose to the throne. His dream had always been that of conquering Constantinople. The siege began on April 5, 1453, and on the morning of May 23rd the city surrendered. Christian Constantinople thus passed into the hands of a sultan barely 23 years old. Later the new city was also to have a different name, Istanbul, an abbreviated form of the Greek expression "eis ten polìn" meaning "towards the city".

The power of the Ottoman empire reached its zenith with Süleyman the Magnificent, whose great architect Sinan embellished the city with magnificent mosques, bridges, palaces, fountains. With the progressive decline of Ottoman power and the dismembering of the empire. the city too declined, until at the dawn of the 20th century the empire came to an end and the young Turkish republic was born. In 1923 the capital was transferred to Ankara, but it is in Istanbul and its glorious monuments that its thousand years of history will live on.

Exterior and interior of the famous Sultanhamet: the Blue Mosque is the only one in the world with six minarets.

BLUE MOSQUE

No one who has been to Istanbul at least once can ever forget the feeling of awe and wonder inspired by the sight of the slender minarets boldly silhouetted against the sky, the looming bulk, the cascade of domes and half domes, the astonishing harmony of its colors and forms. The view is incomparable either from Galata Bridge or from the Golden Horn. Sultan Ahmed's mosque stands firmly opposite Hagia Sophia as if it were trying to rival it in size and grandeur.

Sultan Ahmed I, who came to the throne when he was barely fourteen, was deeply religious and entrusted the construction to a pupil of the great Sinan, the architect Mohammed Ağa, known also as "Sedefkâr", which means "worker of mother-of-pearl". According to a manuscript in the Topkapı library he was originally a gardener in the mausoleum of Süleyman's mosque. He had joined the Janissaries and had dedicated himself to the building of mosques, palaces and fountains,

even going so far as to restore the Kaaba.

Work on the mosque began in 1609 and ended in 1616, just a year before the death of the sultan who had spent 1,181 gold thalers on it. It is said that on the day of the solemn inauguration Ahmed I, as a sign of humility, wore a hat in the shape of the Prophet's foot. The first thing that strikes us as we approach the mosque is that it is the only one in the world to have six minarets, four of which have three balconies each. When the building was finished, the sultan had to add a seventh minaret to the mosque of the Mecca which also had six in order to reestablish its religious primacy.

The mosque is surrounded on three sides by a vast walled courtyard with a portico. Three impressive entrance doors lead into an internal court, paved in marble, which is as large as the inside of the mosque. In the center of the court is the hexagonal *şadirvan* (basin or fountain for ritual ablutions) surrounded by six marble columns.

The inside is approximately square: a single immense space into which the light pours from 260 windows, freely playing over the surfaces. The powerful dome, 43 meters high, is supported by four enormous circular pillars 5 meters in diameter which have vertical grooves and are known as "elephant feet". The mosque takes its name from the splendid blue decoration which covers this perfectly balanced harmonious ensemble. For a third of their height the walls and pillars are sheathed with 21,043 faience tiles of the 16th and 17th centuries, predominantly in all possible shades of blue and with floral designs ranging from roses to tulips, carnations and lilacs.

The pulpit in white marble (mimbar) and the prayer niche (mihrab) oriented towards Mecca.

Sound and light performance on the Blue Mosque.

The Hippodrome, with the obelisk of Theodosius and the walled obelisk.

HIPPODROME

The vast area covered by the Hippodrome lies between Hagia Sophia and the Blue Mosque. It is also known as At Meydani, or plaza of the horses, because after the conquest of Costantinople it was used principally for horse races.

Its original layout dates to 203 A.D. under Septimius Severus. It was enlarged and embellished by Constantine in 325 and recalls the Circus Maximus in Rome. Almost 400 meters long and 120 meters wide, there was room for 100,000 spectators in forty rows of seats. The athleltes were divided into factions: the Blues, the Greens, the Reds, and the Whites. The emperor's box, decorated with four splendid bronze horses which are now in Venice, was to the north. But the plaza of the horses was not the scene of games and festivities only. In 532, during the Ides of January, the revolt against Justinian was staged here. At the cry of nika (which in Greek means "victory"), the rebels raged through the city pillaging and plundering. The uprising, which went down in history as the Nika riots, was bloodily put down by General Belisarius who had over 40,000 men executed next to what was known from then on as the "gate of death". In 1826 the Hippodrome was once more the scene for the execution of 30,000 Janis-saries who had opposed the rule of Sultan Mahmud II. The Hippodrome was so resplendent with statues, obelisks and trophies which came from various countries that St. Jerome wrote: "the splendor of Constantinople is inaugurated despoiling all other cities".

The oldest is without doubt the **obelisk of Theodosius**, a porphyry monolith 25 meters high from Karnak where it had been erected in honor of Thutmosis III. The marble base is 6 meters high and is decorated with low reliefs. Another obelisk is that of Constantine, better known as the **walled obelisk**, which is compared to the Colossus of Rhodes in the inscription on is base. It is 32 meters high and is built of blocks of limestone faced with plaques of gilded bronze and was erected under Constantine VII Porphyrogenitus. The oddest monument is without doubt the **Serpentine Column**, originally 8 meters high (today five and a half meters are left). This bronze column came from Delphi where it had been set up in the temple of Apollo in memory of the victorious battles of Salamina and Platea. It is said that the bodies of the three entwined serpents which form the column were cast from the shields of the Persian soldiers who fell in battle. Lastly the **Kaiser Fountain**, a gift of the German emperor William II to Sultan Abdülhamid II in 1895, during the Kaiser's trip to the East.

The impressive bulk of Hagia Sophia acts as a backdrop for the vast square in front.

HAGIA SOPHIA

Hagia Sophia or the Church of Divine Wisdom is a masterpiece of grandeur and proportions, coveted by the Islamic East and the Christian West, and one of the most important attestations of humanity — surely the only one that for 1400 years has served God and Allah, the Christian world and Islam.

The first church was built between 325 and 360 under Constans II, even though his father Constantine may have had the foundations laid. Ravaged by fire in 404, it was restored and reconsecrated by Theodosius II only to be completely burnt down during the Nika riots in January 532. Justinian had only recently risen to the throne and the supreme ambition of the emperor, a champion of the cause of orthodox Christianity and divinely appointed, was to build the greatest temple that Christianity had ever had. No more than 32 days had elapsed after the destruction of the church when work on the new building began. It is said that the shape of the church was revealed to Justinian in a dream. Artisans arrived from all parts of the world. Justinian, who spent much of his time in the building yards, named one hundred overseers, each one responsible for a hundred workers. Anthemios of Tralles was designated as architect in chief, assisted by Isidoros of Miletos, both Greeks from Asia Minor. On December 27, 537, Hagia Sophia was solemnly consecrated by the emperor. It is said that when he arrived in front of the church, Justinian raised his arms to heaven and exclaimed "Glory to God who has deigned to let me finish so great a work. O Solomon, I have outdone thee!''. And indeed Hagia Sophia seems to surpass Solomon's temple in size, beauty and richness. The grand interior of the basilica is central plan. With a total surface of 7,570 square meters, Hagia Sophia takes fourth place after St. Peter's, the Cathedral of Seville and that of Milan. The interior is dominated by the enormous dome 55 meters above the ground and with a diameter of over 36 meters. Forty ribs divide the dome into sections which terminate at their base in 40 windows. The weight of the dome is supported by four main pillars which in turn are buttressed by four smaller pillars. Hagia Sophia was also an exultation of light which entered through the numerous windows to illuminate the nave where the worshippers were gathered in prayer. At night thousands of lamps and candelabra reflected their light on the 16,000 square meters of gold mosaics scattered here and there throughout the building. The dome too was covered by a pure gold mosaic, with a cross at the center. Unfortunately most of the mosaic decoration of Hagia Sophia disappeared, first under the wrath of the iconoclasts, who spared only the abstract decoration, and subsequently with the conquest of the Ottoman

Turks and the Islamic prohibition to reproduce the human figure. Natural calamities sorely tried the architectural challenge of Hagia Sophia. The earthquakes of 553 and 557 weakened the structure of the basilica, until in 558 the eastern arch and part of the dome crashed to the ground destroying the altar, the ciborium and the ambo. Restored and newly consecrated, Hagia Sophia was to see other more tragic events.

At the beginning of the 13th century Constantinople, after having withstood at least seventeen sieges by barbarians and infidels, fell under the fury of a Christian army. During the three days of plunder, Hagia Sophia was completely pillaged and stripped of its precious icons, its gold and silver candelabra, the jeweled crosses, the glittering reliquaries. Anything of gold was simply melted down. On May 29, 1453 the Ottoman Turks conquered Costantinople. That day, late in the afternoon, Mohammed II entered Hagia Sophia and for the first time after nine centuries, the imam's prayer to Allah, the only god, resounded under the imposing domes. The transformation of Hagia Sophia into a mosque was carried out with unbelievable respect,

The majestic interior of the church: the large wooden disks have the names of Allah, Mohammed and the first four prophets in gilded lettering on a green ground.

Christ the Pantocrator flanked by the Empress Zoë and her third husband Constantine IX Monomachus in an 11th-century mosaic.

Mausoleum of Selim II, the sultan defeated in the famous battle of Lepanto.

The Virgin and Child between the Emperor John II Comnenus and his wife Irene. To be noted the complicated hairdress of the empress.

even though there were of course many changes. The metal cross on the dome was replaced by the crescent moon which a century later was covered — it is said — with 50,000 fused gold coins. The ambo was replaced by a mimbar, and a mihrab for prayer in the direction of Mecca was set up. An initial polygonal minaret was built to which others were later added. But the icons, the iconostasis, and various Christian mosaic with human figures were not touched.

The exterior of Hagia Sophia was also modified. What had been the baptistery was transformed at the beginning of the 17th century into the turbeh of Mustafa I, where this sultan is buried together with his nephew Ibrahim. Next to this mausoleum are the octagonal

and hexagonal tombs of three other sultans, Mohammed III, Selim II and Murat III, each with their wives and relatives.

The 20th century brought the downfall of the Ottoman Empire and the simultaneous rise of the young Turkish republic.

The first president, Kemal Atatürk, decided to transform the mosque into a Byzantine-Ottoman museum and in April 1932 the mosaics once more began to be laid bare: so it was that, under the careful guidance of Thomas Whittemore of the Byzantine Institute of America the gleaming gold mosaics began to surface from the walls of the mosque, direct evidence of the great past of Hagia Sophia and of the city as a whole.

15

The Ortakapı, the central gateway leading to the Topkapı Saray.

PALACE OF TOPKAPI

The Palace of Topkapı, or Topkapı Saray, is an extraordinary complex of buildings spread out over one of the seven hills of Istanbul, in a splendid site above the Sea of Marmara and the Golden Horn. Constantine's imperial palace once stood here until it was abandoned and fell into ruin with the fall of the Empire. When the Turks conquered Istanbul, Mohammed II first chose the site of the present University as the seat for his palace, but later decided to rebuild the palace of Topkapı, which means "gate of the cannon". Begun in 1462, its principal parts were finished in 1478 and it was the official seat of the Ottoman sultans up until 1855 when Abdülmecid moved to the new and sumptuous palace of Dolmabahçe, built on the

model of the ostentatious imperial residences of the west.

We enter the palace through the Ortakapi, the central gate known also as Bâb-ı-Salaam, or "gate of salvation". Built in 1525 under Süleyman the Magnificent, it is flanked by two octagonal gates where those condemned to death were kept prisoner. Only the sultan could pass through Bâb-ı-Salaam on horseback — all the others had to go on foot.

Immediately behind the entrance we find the beautiful kitchens built at the time of Mohammed the Conqueror and later restored by Sinan. They are a strange imposing sight: each one is composed of two square rooms covered with a dome with eight windows and topped by ten conical chimneys. A splendid collection of Chinese and Japanese porcelain is now exhibited here where once 1200 cooks were kept at work.

TREASURY — *By general consensus one of the most fascinating parts of Topkapı: in these rooms jewels and objects of incomparable beauty and inestimable worth which belonged to the sultans are on display.*

Throne of Nadir — Known also as the throne of Shah Ismail (it is thought to have belonged to him), it is basically an oval armchair on four legs 46 cm. high, made of ebony covered with gold, and with emeralds, rubies and pearls set into a layer of enamel. Along the outer border of the throne there are nine pine cones of rubies crowned by an emerald. The pillow, in purple velvet, is decorated with plaques of gold with flowers in pearls, rubies and turquoises. A costly work of Indian craftsmanship, it was brought back as war booty by Nadir Shah and presented to Sultan Mahmud I as a gift in 1746. Since it comes from India some scholars have even advanced the fascinating hypothesis that this precious throne belonged to no less a person than Tamerlane.

Dagger — This splendid jewel, so famous that it was even the protagonist of a celebrated film, was one of the gifts that Sultan Mahmud I sent to Nadir Shah in 1746. When the Turkish delegation arrived in Baghdad, they had news of a bloody revolution in Persia in which the shah himself had been killed. The Turkish ambassadors returned to Istanbul, taking all their gifts with them, including the dagger. It is 35 cm. long and encrusted with diamonds and with enamel decoration representing bowls of fruit on both sides. The hilt consists of three enormous emeralds surrounded by diamonds. Another octagonal cut emerald, which closes on a small watch, is at the tip of the hilt.

The "spoon" diamond — A jewel from A Thousand and One Nights, this diamond of 86 karats is surrounded by forty-nine extremely pure cut diamonds. There are two constrasting versions as to the stone's origin. The first, perhaps a legend, says that it was found in a refuse heap by a poor fisherman who sold it to a crafty jeweler in the bazaar in exchange for three spoons. This explains the name of the diamond, "kaşikçi", which in Turkish means "maker of spoons", although the jewel also recalls a spoon in its form. According to the second version which is certainly much more reliable, a French officer named Pigot bought it in 1774 from the Maharajah of Madras and took it to France. It changed hands several times and was put on auction, in which Giacomo Casanova is also said to have taken part, and was acquired by Napoleon's mother who however had to sell it in an attempt to save her son from exile. Then, for 150,000 gold coins it came into the possession of the governor Tepedelenli Alì Paşa who put it with the other jewels in his personal treasury.

When the governor was accused of treason and dismissed by Mahmud II, the diamond became part of the Ottoman treasury. It also seems likely that this diamond is the Pikot diamond, all track of which has been lost and which was also said to have been 86 karats.

Ceremonial throne — The throne that the Turkish sultans used during the solemn investiture ceremonies is 178 cm. high and is in walnut completely sheathed with golden plaques for which 80,000 golden ducats where melted down.

It weighs 250 kilograms and 954 chrysolites are embedded in it. In 1585 it was presented to Murat III by the governor of Egypt Ibrahim Paşa and remained in the Topkapı palace even after the sultans had moved to the palace of Dolmabahçe.

HAREM

HAREM — The word harem derives from the Arab "harim" which means something forbidden and "haram", literally sanctuary. The harem was in fact the private residence of the sultan, the quarter where the women in the palace lived — the Turkish sovereign's mother, his sister, his wives, his concubines.. The harem today covers an area of circa 15,000 square meters: it was governed by a corps of black eunuchs, almost all Abyssinians who had been offered to the Sultan by the pasha of Egypt when they were young. They guarded the entrances to the harem so that no outsider might enter the apartments reserved to the women.

Twin pavilions — Known also as the "Apartments of the heir" they are two communicating rooms facing on the courtyard of the favorites and the pool of the concubines. The 17th-century ceramics on the walls represent tulips, roses, hyacinths, cypresses.

Imperial Hall — This is the largest room in the harem, begun under Süleyman the Magnificent by Sinan but radically changed in 1750 with the insertion of mirrors which conceal secret doors, of wainscotting, and marble columns. In this spacious place, lighted by twenty-six windows, the sultan and the women of the harem participated in parties, balls and entertainment.

The fireplace and a corner of the Twin Pavilions.

Two views of the luxurious Imperial Hall.

The Mosque of Süleyman, by Sinan, never fails to astound for the solennity of its appearance and its imposing proportions.

MOSQUE OF SULTAN SÜLEYMAN

Built by the great Sinan for Süleyman the Magnificent between 1550 and 1557, it has four slender minarets on the outside, a symbol that Süleyman was the fourth Ottoman sultan, while the ten galleries which run along the minarets refer to the fact that he was the tenth sultan of the reigning dynasty.

The interior is truly overwhelming in the grandeur of its proportions, the austerity of its aspect, the absence of any excessive ornamentation. Almost square, it is dominated by an enormous dome on a drum, 53 meters high. One hundred and thirty-eight windows flood the hall with variegated light. The only decorative elements are the lovely inscriptions by Ahmed Karahisari, one of the greatest 16th-century Turkish calligraphers, and the elegant white-ground ceramic tiles with flowers and leaves in turquoise, blue, and red, from the kilns in Iznik, ancient Nicaea, famous not only for the two councils held there but also for its ceramic art.

Türbeh of Süleyman the Magnificent — Behind the mosque, in a small cementery is the türbeh of Süleyman, which may also be by Sinan. Octagonal in form, the dome is supported by eight slender porphyry columns. Here the great sultan, who died in 1566 at the age of 71, reposes on an imposing catafalque, next to his daughter Mihrimah and the other two sovereigns, Süleyman II and Ahmed II. Nearby, another mausoleum, also octagonal in shape, belongs to Roxelane, literally the Russian, because that is where she was supposedly from. She was the great Süleyman's favorite: for her he repudiated all the other women in his harem and gave her the name of Hürrem, the "laughing one".

In the Covered Bazaar of Istanbul
the shop windows of jewelers
alternate with others
displaying the typical objects
in brassware.

GREAT
BAZAAR

The great covered Bazaar of Istanbul, the Kapalı Çarşı,is not simply a complex of buildings but a real city covered by hemispheric domes with its streets, its small squares surrounded by porticoes, its entrances (18 in all), 5 mosques, 6 fountains. Its 200,000 square meters make it one of the largest souks in the world. In Byzantine times venders already set up their stalls here. Then in 1461 Mohammed the Conqueror built the first covered bazaar in wood which was destroyed by fire more than once until it was finally rebuilt in stone.

GALATA BRIDGE

The bridge, 468 meters long and 26 meters wide, rests on twenty-two pontoons and is the real pulsating center of Istanbul — variegated, noisy, lively, always crowded with pedlars and fishermen, with shops and typical seafood restaurants which open off the arcades.

At night, between two and four, the central part of the bridge opens and turns so that ships can pass through. The bridge was originally in wood, and was built in 1835 on the orders of the Sultana Bezmi Alem, mother of Abdülmecid. In 1877 it was replaced by the present bridge in iron.

Galata Bridge seen from a minaret of the Yani Camii, or New Mosque.

*An enchanting view of the Bosphorus from the
Rumeli Hisari.*

RUMELI HISARI

The name of this imposing fortress, one of the most beautiful and enchanting spots on the Bosporus, means "fortress of Europe". In fact the Turks use the word Rumeli to refer to the part on the European shore and Anadolu for the part on the Asian shore. Begun in 1452, a year before the conquest of Constantinople, by Mohammed II, it took more than 3,000 workers only three months to build. Before launching the decisive attack on the city the sultan, who had by this time surrounded the Byzantine capital on all sides, wanted to be sure of the passage in the narrowest point of the Bosporus, so as to impede the arrival of aid from the Black Sea or any attempts at flight in that direction. Not only did he succeed in his intentions, but at the same time he acquired the sole rights to collect toll from all ships that wanted to cross the strait. Now, in summer, in the shade of its crenellated walls and circular towers, important performances of classic theatre are given here.

The internal courtyard of the Eyüp Mosque.

EYÜP MOSQUE

Not only is it considered the holy mosque of Istanbul but, after Mecca and Jerusalem, it may even be the third holy place for pilgrims in the Islamic world. Its fame lies in the fact that this is the burial place of the standard bearer of the prophet Mohammed, Eyüp-ül-Ensârî-Halit Bin Zeyd, who was struck down and buried in the battle field during the first siege of Costantinople by the Arabs in 669. At the time of the great siege, in 1453, the story goes that Mohammed the Conqueror saw in a dream the place where Eyüp was buried. When he had the spot dug up he found what he had seen in his dream. The sultan then had a mosque built, which soon became the object of pilgrimages and a place of worship. Every time a sultan mounted the throne it was here that the ceremony of the conferral of the new sword was held and the newly elected sultan was girded with the sword of Osman, symbol of the caliphate.

27

Panorama of Bursa, the ancient Prusia, resting at the foot of Mount Olympus.

BURSA

One of the most important cities in Turkey, with a significant architectural and artistic patrimony, Bursa lies on the northwest slopes of Mt. Ulu Dağ, once known as the *Mount Olympus of Misia*. The closeness of the southern riviera of the Sea of Marmara and the presence of curative hot springs, long known and exploited, make Bursa one of the most popular cities for foreign visitors.

The territory where the present city stands was settled in earliest times, and was eventually taken over by Cyrus (6th cent. B.C.). It later became a Roman colony, and afterwards a flourishing center for Christianity, which was introduced by the apostle Andrew, as well as an active center for trade, thanks to its geographical site at the junction of important trade routes. When it passed under Byzantine control, it long resisted the Seljuk attempts at conquest, and finally surrendered to the Ottoman armies in the first half of the 14th century. As long as it was capital of the empire its importance grew, but when the capital was transferred, first to Hadrianopolis and then to Constantinople, decline was inevitable.

The most famous building in Bursa is the **Yesil Camii** or *Green Mosque*, built early in the 15th century together with the nearby **Yesil Türbeh** (*Green Mausoleum*) by Mehmet I Çelebi. Thanks to restoration the mosque has regained its original splendor, enabling the public to admire the splendid turquoise-blue tiles which give the complex its name. The Green Mausoleum has an octagonal ground plan and is co-

The Ulu Camii, or Great Mosque, and the Yesil Türbeh, or Green Mausoleum.

vered by a conical dome. Built to house the mortal remains of Mehmet I Çelebi, its most striking architectural features are those which distinguish it from the usual type of Ottoman funerary building, and confer an aspect of manifest clarity to the ensemble.

The **Ulu Camii** or *Great Mosque* was built over a period of time that ranges from the second half of the 14th century to the first half of the 15th. Extremely lucid structurally, its twenty small domes make it highly visible. Other outstanding elements include a wooden *mimbar*, the *mihrab*, unfortunately altered by later interventions, the *sadirvan* (lustral fountain) and an interesting library with rare and valuable manuscripts.

Nor should the **Bayazit Camii**, built at the turn of the 14th century, be overlooked. Its innovative architectural plan in the shape of an upturned T was to be canonized in the later religious architecture of the city. Also of note are the **Orhan Camii** (15th cent.), the **Emir Sultan Camii**, rebuilt in the early 19th century after the original building had been struck by an earthquake, and the **Muradiye Camii**, 15th century, striking for its ceramic decor and with the sepulchral monuments of the sovereign, his family and others belonging to the sultanate in the garden.

The old historical center (*Hisar*) stands on the site of the fortified structures dating to the Roman and Byzantine periods, of which a few bulwarks are still extant.

The ancient fame of Bursa as a spa is spoken for by what remains of the venerable complex of **Eski Kaplica** installed in the 14th century on the site of pre-existing spa structures dating to the period of Justinian. The persistence of some of the architectural elements of that time documents the antiquity of these mineral springs and the fact that they were used long ago. The most recent spa complex dates to the 16th-17th century; it is named **Yenı Kaplica** and is attributed to the grand vizier of Süleyman the Magnificent. Of particular interest are the fine marble pavements and the blue majolica decorations.

Ulu Dağ, the ancient Mount Olympus, is today one of the best equipped winter sport resorts.

*Canakkale, in a highly strategic position, controlled
the Strait of the Dardanelles.*

CANAKKALE

From a strategic and military point of view this small town is of major importance for it guards the entire strait of the Dardanelles (*Canakkale Bogazi*) at its narrowest point.

While the strait of the Dardanelles which joins the Aegean to the Sea of Marmara was known in antiquity as *Hellespont*, its present name is related to the myth of Dardanus, the legendary founder of Troy. Its enormous strategical importance has always made it the object of attention on the part of the emerging powers. More recently attention centered on Canakkale as a result of the dispute which arose when, in September of 1922, a small garrison of British soldiers found themselves confronted with the troops of Mustafà Kemal. Open war between the two countries was avoided only when Britain's ex-allies explicitly refused military intervention against Mustafà Kemal's soldiers. In the following month a preliminary agreement between the two parties paved the way for the treaty of Lausanne which was signed in 1923 and which allowed Turkey to annex extensive areas.

From their heights the ruins of Troy overlook the valley where Homer's heroes fought their great battles.

TROY

The fascinating remains of this unique city, whose origins are veiled in myth and legend, are visible in a limited area situated to the south of the strait of the Dardanelles, between the flood plain furrowed by the waters of the Küçük Menderes and the hilly ramparts of Hisarlik. At least in part, the conspicuous remains of an ancient city that came to light in the archaeological excavations begun in the middle of the 19th century fit the description of the legendary *Ilium* celebrated in the famous epic poem.

In 1870 the German archaeologist Heinrich Schliemann began the first trial digs, convinced of the existence of a city near Hisarlik, in open disagreement with those who up till then had maintained that Troy was nothing but a myth sung by Homer. After his death, work was continued by Wilhelm Dörpfeld until

1894. Excavations were resumed by Carl W. Blegen, confirming the existence, all told, of nine levels of cities (*Troy I-IX*).

The first settlements, dating to around 3000 B.C., refer to the existence of a large fortified structure. The phase known as *Troy I* lasted about five centuries and ended with a fire. *Troy II*, larger and more evolved, was also burned to the ground. Nothing basically new is revealed in the successive Bronze Age settlements, at least until the phase known as *Troy VI*, the period of greatest splendor in the complex vicissitudes of Troy. Around 1300 B.C. the city was struck by a serious earthquake. It was immediately rebuilt and gave us what we know as *Troy VIIa*, identified by scholars as the legendary city described in the Iliad. Tradition indicates 1184 B.C. as the year in which classic Troy fell,

A corner of the fortifications in the excavations of ancient Troy.

An imaginary reconstruction of the wooden horse the Greeks used to capture Troy.

and archaeological evidence also dates the end of this phase around 1200 B.C., followed immediately by the one known as *Troy VIIb* (1200-1100 B.C.) . After a long period of abandon, the old location was once more settled in 700 B.C., when a small village rose on the site of the Bronze Age fortifications. The phase *Troy IX* refers to the Hellenistic and Roman periods. After this began a slow but inexorable period of decadence and degradation which climaxed in the disappearance of the city around the 5th century A.D. All trace of Troy then vanished and the city, lost and forgotten, survived solely in the pages of Homer until Schliemann's sensational discovery which constitutes one of the fundamental pages in the history of modern and contemporary archaeology.

ASSOS

The ruins of the ancient Greek city of Assos, now known as *Behramkov*, are laid out around a rocky hillside, facing the narrow ocean inlet which separates this stretch of the ancient Troad from the Greek island of Lesbos.

These sites were first colonized by Greek colonists from what is now Mithimmna, on the island of Lesbos. In the 6th century B.C. the locality passed under the sovereignty of Lydia, eventually becoming part of the Persian province of Phrygia and the Hellespont. In 385 B.C. Artaxerxes, king of the Persians, defeated the rebel forces led by the governor of the place, at Assos. Around the 4th century B.C. it was a flourishing intellectual center with a particularly keen philosophical activity thanks to the presence of Aristotle himself and of Cleanthes of Assos, one of the founders of the so-called "Stoic School". In the 3rd and 2nd centuries B.C. Assos became part of the territories controlled by the kingdom of Pergamon.

Archaeological exploration, begun in the second half of the 19th century by J. T. Clarke and F. H. Bacon, has uncovered the remains of an imposing *defensive wall*, enumerated among the most impressive evidences of the Greek world (4th cent. B.C.). The **Temple of Athena**, of which unfortunately only a few scattered traces remain, was built around 530 B.C. on the highest part of the acropolis. Originally in Doric style, it reveals Ionic superpositions; the outline of the stylobate can still be followed, surrounded by a row of 13 columns on the long sides and 6 on each short side. Along the terraces that slope down from the acropolis can be seen what is left of the *Agora*, the *Gymnasium* and a *Theatre*. North of the acropolis stands a *Mosque* erected by the Turks in the time of Murat I (14th cent.).

Overlooking the sea, all that remains of the Temple of Athena in Assos.

Two pictures of modern Ankara.

ANKARA

The capital of modern Turkey is situated at the heart of the extensive Anatolian plateau, at the foot of the mountain chain known as Elma Dağı, point of encounter for a radiating system of important communication routes.

In spite of its basically modern appearance, with new buildings and wide streets where traffic flows smoothly, the origins of Ankara go far back in time. While numerous prehistoric sites have been identified in the environs, the precise location where man unquestionably settled as far back as the Hittite period has still to be established. Funerary material, datable to the Phrygian period and a great number of tumuli testify to the existence of a necropolis that must have served a Phrygian center of considerable size, between the 8th and the 6th century B.C. Around the middle of the 3rd century B.C. the city was occupied by the Galatians who were subjugated by Augustus in 25 A.D. Ancient *Ancyra* (later Angora), a center for the production of angora wool which is still of economic importance for the textile industry, was taken over by the Seljuk Turks in 1147. The fortunes of modern Ankara. second only to Istanbul in population, can be attributed in great

Exterior of the Mausoleum of Atatürk.

part to Mustafà Kemal, better known as *Atatürk* (the "Father of the Turks"), who created the modern state of Turkey and promoted and encouraged the process of westernization, bringing Turkey much closer to Europe than the purely geographical distances might seem to indicate.

The **Museum of Anatolian Cultures** in Ankara can be numbered among the most interesting museum collections in all of Turkey, in particular as far as the material regarding the ancient civilization of the Hittites is concerned. The museum has been installed in two 15th-century buildings, one of which is attributed to Mahmut Pasha, one of the grand viziers of Mehmet II, who included the city of Constantinople in his possessions. The two buildings are intercommunicating and have a roof with ten domes. The collections range from prehistory through the Hittite, Phrygian, Urartian, Persian, Greek and Roman civilizations. Of particular importance is the material that documents the arts and crafts of the Hittites dating as far back as 6000 B.C., in addition to bronzes, objects in sandstone, pottery, a bust of Trajan of the period of the Empire, jewelry, bas-reliefs and an immense quantity of other objects. This enormous mass of material comes from the archaeological sites of Ankara itself, Acemhöyük, Alacahöyük, Alişar, Altintepe, Beyce Sultan, Bogaz-köy, Can Hasan, Çatalhöyük, Eskiyapar Gordion, Hacilar, Kargamis, Kültepe, Ikiztepe, Inandik, Malatya, Pazarli, Patnos, Sakçegözü, Toprakkale and is of invaluable aid in an attempt to fully understand the complex cultural and artistic vicissitudes of the Anatolian region.

The vestiges of the ancient **Citadel** composed of a double circuit of walls around the agora can still be identified on the hill named *Hisar* which rises up near the museum. The agora dates to the Greek and Roman periods, while the first structures of the complex fortifications were built under Galatian domination. The complex of narrow lanes is particularly picturesque, and fragments of architecture and sculpture dating to Roman times can, not infrequently, be observed.

Among the most representative examples of Roman honorary architecture in the city, the **Temple of Augustus** became particularly meaningful with the discovery, in the second half of the 16th century, of the so-called *Monumentum Ancyranum*, a bilingual inscription in Latin and Greek which constitutes a sort of spiritual testament of the great emperor. What remains of the temple has come down to us in fairly good condition. The building seems to have been erected in the 2nd century B.C. and appears to have initially been dedicated to the cult of Cybele. Other sources

The Calidarium of the Roman Baths, built in the 3rd century A.D., perhaps by Caracalla.

The Column of Julian, or minaret of the Queen of Saba, possibly erected in 362 and 15 meters high.

maintain that it was built when Augustus added the Galatian province to the empire, just after 25 B.C. Even though nothing is left of the covering, the architrave or the imposing colonnade, there is reason to think that the temple was surrounded by Ionic columns (*peristasis*; 8 on the short sides and 15 on the long sides). When it was transformed into a Christian church in the Byzantine period, substantial architectural changes were made. The **Hacı Bayram Camii** was raised next to the northwest corner of the temple at the beginning of the 15th century, when the city fell into the hands of the Turks. This mosque in brick and stone is to be noted for its fine interior decor, the fruit of an 18th-century superposition.

Not far from the so-called **Column of Julian**, an interesting object with a capital in Byzantine style (raised in the second half of the 4th century to honor Julian the Apostate's visit to Ancyra, are the **Roman Baths**. What little is left of the bath complex suffices to document the existence of a large establishment, of which the remains of a *palaestra*, a *piscina* and rooms heated by various furnaces are still visible.

The **Mausoleum of Atatürk** is set at the top of a hill overlooking a scenic boulevard, flanked by granite statues of lions, which leads to a square at the base of the monumental staircase.

The building is one of the finest expressions of contemporary Turkish honorary architecture. It was built between the middle of the 1940s and the early 50s by the architects Orhan Arda and Emin Onat, and constitutes one of the most interesting sights for visitors to the capital. This fine piece of architecture is in travertine, richly decorated inside with marble and mosaics; the bronze doors were cast in Italy. The mortal remains of Mustafà Kemal lie in the crypt under the cenotaph, while the wings of the monumental complex house a museum documenting the life and works of the great Turkish statesman. Other places to which the memory of Atatürk is bound include the *house* where he lived during the wars for national independence and a *museum* with numerous relics and keepsakes.

Outstanding among the mosques in the Turkish capital is the one known as **Arslanhane Camii.** The oldest Muslim place of worship in the city, it was built early in the

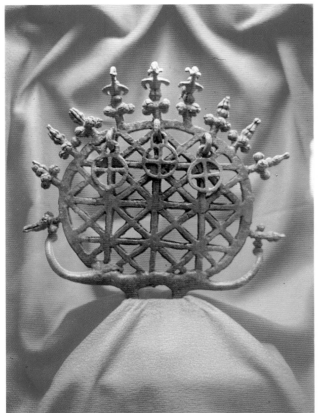

13th century, employing architectural elements taken from earlier Roman and Byzantine buildings. These indications of the past can frequently be identified, generally in the fabric of the mosque. The highly evocative interior has a fine *mimbar* carved in walnut, while the classic *mihrab* reveals its Seljuk origins in the refined decorations of the tiles and the glazes.

Another example of religious architecture in the city is the so-called **New Mosque** (*Yeni Camii*) attributed to the school of the famous Ottoman architect Sinan. The mosque is dated to the 16th century and houses a marble pulpit and a prayer niche, both of which are also of the same period.

Other spots of interest for tourists and visitors to Ankara include the **Ethnographical Museum** with its documentation of local crafts and folklore; the **Maltepe Camii**, an important expression of contemporary religious architecture, with a dome faced in brass and topped by a delicate slender minaret; the 15th-century **Imaret Camii**, built with old Roman materials and flanked by a minaret enhanced by multicolor tiles, as well as numerous public parks, in particular the one for young people (*Gençlik Parki*).

Fragment of a relief in basalt from Karkemish, depicting the goddess Kubaba (9th cent. B.C.).

Relief in basalt of a war chariot: the hairdo of the soldiers reveals Assyrian influence.

The so-called Gate of Lions: lion figures are typical of the Hittite period and date to the 14th-13th century B.C.

BOĞAZKÖY

The vestiges of the mythical city of **Hattushash**, the capital and cradle of Hittite civilization, are scattered over a steep terraced slope that overlooks the houses of Boğazköy.

The first forms of human settlement certainly date to pre-Hittite times around 2500 B.C. The place name Hattushash derives, with all probability, from *Hatti*, the name of the people who settled here in pre-Hittite times. At the height of its splendor the Hittite civilization became so powerful as to present a military threat to Babylonia which it eventually subjugated. The decline of the Hittites, worn out by varying attempts at conquest, began with the destruction of Hattushash around the middle of the 14th century B.C. Two centuries later the Hittite empire was unquestionably in its death throes and fire was set to the ancient capital by the Phrygians.

The first archaelogical excavations discovered interesting fragments with examples of cuneiform writing near the so-called *Great Temple*. It was not until 1915 that the Czech linguist F. Hrozny discovered the key to deciphering the Hittite alphabet.

The Great Temple, known also as **Temple of the God of Tempests and the Goddess of the Sun**, is undoubtedly one of the most frequently visited tourist attractions. It is dated in the 13th century B.C. and the vast area covered by the ruins gives us an idea of the original complex which consisted of a central sanctuary surrounded by rows of rooms and halls used for archives (this was where the examples of cuneiform writing mentioned above were found in 1907) and storerooms which still contained a great number of amphoras.

The topmost part of the acropolis is occupied by the majestic ruins of the **Büyükkale** or *Great Citadel*, entrance to which is through the so-called **Gate of Lions**, flanked by two lions in hard basalt. The Citadel complex contained the living quarters of the Hittite sovereigns and a number of rooms to be used by the public, including one thought to have been a library from which numerous examples of cuneiform writing have come, and in particular a baked clay tablet incised with the *Treaty of Kadesh*, stipulated between the Hittites and the Egyptians in 1279 B.C.

The various entrance gates set into the circuit of the imposing Hittite walls give us an idea of the skill these people had developed in the field of military architecture. One of these is the **Royal Gate**, whose construction dates to the beginnings of the 14th century B.C. and which also furnished an interesting relief, now in the Archaeological Museum of Ankara.

YAZILIKAYA

The emblematic rock-cut sanctuary of Yazılıkaya is a sort of pantheon of the Hittite divinities. Large numbers of tourists combine an outing to the excavations of Hattushash, not much more than two km. distant, with a visit to this evocative open-air site in its harsh natural surroundings.

It is likely that a precedent place of worship, presumably of Hurrite extraction, already existed on the spot where the ruins of the Hittite temple and magnificent bas-reliefs carved into the living rock now stand. The origins of the Hittite temple, which does however have diverse building levels, seem to date at least as far back as the middle of the 13th century B.C.

Archaeological investigation, still in course, has not yet found an exact explanation for the uncovered room, recently brought to light near the smaller of the two galleries carved with bas-reliefs. The west wall of the larger gallery is ornamented with low reliefs of male divinities while those on the east wall represent female divinities. This differentiation according to sex is not, however, absolute, for at least three female divinities appear in the sequence of gods, while one male divinity is to be found in the row of goddesses. The two rows meet on the north wall where the most important images in the shrine of Yazılıkaya are to be found: the God of Tempests *Teshub* and the Goddess of the Sun *Hepatu*. The largest relief in the main gallery however is the one representing King *Tudhaliyas IV*, thus giving us a date in the second half of the 13th century B.C. The figure of this king is directly related to the chronology of this unique sanctuary, built by Hattusilis III and his consort Puduhepa (1275-1250 B.C.), father and mother of the above named king.

There are also splendid extremely well-preserved bas-reliefs in the smaller gallery, which archaeologists generally think was connected with the cult of a deceased king (Tudhaliyas II or III). Even so reasons exist to support the supposition that the gallery may also have served to exalt the personality cult of Tudhaliyas IV while he was still living. This is corroborated by the fact that his figure occupies an important place in the larger gallery and is repeated at least twice in the lesser gallery, where one can admire the famous representation of the sovereign embraced by the god *Sharruma*, a sign of protection, and one of the finest stylistic motifs of the entire cycle of Yazılıkaya.

Two pictures of the famous rock-cut sanctuary of Yazılıkaya. The relief on one side of the rock depicts the god Sarruma and King Tudhaliyas IV, and on the other the so-called "twelve blessed ones", a procession of minor gods in the Hittite pantheon. Both reliefs date to 1250-1220 B.C.

The monumental Gate of Sphinxes in Alaca Hüyük.

ALACA HÜYÜK

The interesting archaeological site of Alaca Hüyük is situated at the northern tip of an imaginary triangle which joins the most important tourist attractions, in the area around the village of Bogazkale or Boğazköy. The spot where the ancient ruins lie was settled in the dawn of prehistory, even before the early Bronze Age, and then by the Hittites and others. Some hypotheses (far however from being proved) affirm that this was the site of Kussara, a city the Hittites had already established around 4000 B.C. before the capital was transferred to Hattushash.

The first excavations in the territory of Alaca Hüyük were carried out in the first half of the 19th century. Further investigation was undertaken at the beginning of the 20th century for the Museum of Istanbul, even though a real excavation campaign did not get under way until the middle of the 1930s. Archaeological explorations personally initiated by Atatürk and directed by Remzi Oğuz Arik and Hamit Z. Koşay, for the Historical Association of Turkey, have made it possible to define a series of, all told, fifteen superposed levels, involving different periods and cultures. The period of greatest splendor of the Hittite empire has been identified in the second level which ranges in time from the 21st to the 13th century B.C. The archaeological finds brought to light during the excavations play an important part in the exhibitions of the Museum of Anatolian Cultures in Ankara but the material installed in the local Museum and to be seen throughout the archaeological zone is also plentiful and interesting.

Of particular note for the tourist is the so-called **Gate of Sphinxes**, which leads to the remains of a vast temple structure, similar in size to the one at Boğazköy. The gate mentioned above is actually a copy of the original which has been transferred to the Museum in Ankara. Its historical and artistic importance however is not to be underrated for this man-made object from the time of the Hittite empire (15th-13th cent. B.C.) has a typical Hittite ornamental motif inside the piers, the two-headed eagle, and an element clearly of Egyptian derivation, the sphinx, depicted frontally on both pillars.

Scenic view of Ürgüp.

ÜRGÜP

The town of Ürgüp is on the road from Kayseri to Nevşehir and Aksaray. It is built at the foot of a large, slightly sloping plateau. The oldest dwellings, built againt the crags into which they sometimes penetrate, consist of blocks of local pink and beige tufa, which blend in with the landscape.

In fact, with their flat roofs, buildings are camouflaged against the square jagged rocks that erosion has isolated from the steep slopes of the plateau. Near the ancient village, whose dwellings lie scattered in the plain below, stands a large tourist resort, consisting of a series of modern buildings in keeping with traditional local architecture. In this way, public infrastructures required for the influx of tourists — including a museum — are functional without disturbing the evocative panorama. In fact, the attraction of Ürgüp and outlying villages lies in its unusual geological features. It is

surrounded by wide areas crossed by pinkish gorges near tufa quarries and so-called fairy chimneys which characterize the landscape between Ürgüp and Nevşehir. In fact, they are tall pinnacles of tufa, often with large blocks balanced on top; the rocks, faulted through geological movements, have enabled atmospheric agents to infiltrate between the individual blocks, molding and isolating the pinnacles, which are protected by the rocks balancing on top of them against rainfall.

A matter of kilometers from Ürgüp, numerous churches and chapels are dotted here and there over a vast area; they include the ancient buildings of the Balkan valley (6th century) in the direction of Ortahisar. Near Cemil stands the Basmelek Monastery ("of the Archangel"), whereas Ayvalik boasts the churches of Karaçali and Yucari.

The imposing honeycombed rock in the center of Ortahisar.

Uçhisar, one of the most fascinating sites in Cappadocia.

ORTAHISAR

Ortahisar, or "middle" fortress, is distinguished by a series of buildings which are picturesque in their simplicity. These houses and warehouses — used for storing fruit and vegetables — are usually double-storied; access is gained to the top floor by means of a flight of steps often without a balustrade. More modern buildings are made of the same local stone in masonry; outer surfaces are white-washed and decorated with simple moldings. Therefore the town complex is characterized by extreme simplicity and the similarity of the buildings, usually with flat roofs; in the narrow streets one still comes across carts on four small wheels, equipped with boards and canvas sunshades over the coachman's seat. Near the village square stands a jagged rock similar to a tower, called Sivrikaya; countless rooms have been hewn out inside its peak. It has crumbled in parts, enabling one to see the interiors of some of its rooms and repairs have been done to the original dry wall complex.

UÇHISAR

The triple rock of Uçhisar is near Göreme. At a distance, the town looks as though it is crowned by a rocky skyscraper studded with little windows; in time, some of the walls have been washed away, leaving the rooms inside open to the sky.
The citadel which towers several tens of meters above the town looks like a large cylindrical tower flanked by a pointed fault when seen from the west. In ancient times, a tunnel was hewn for several hundred meters under the houses out of the tufa of the mountain in order to guarantee a water supply in the event of siege. Here too, as in Ortahisar, the modern part of the town is fitted out for tourists; from a nearby hotel, partly built into the rock-face in a particularly scenic area, one can admire both the village in its entirety and its light-colored eroded crags between deep gorges.
Nearby this hotel stands a so-called "pigeon-loft": these buildings are quite frequent in Cappadocia, but here they are even more common. It is a wide stretch

The eerie landscape around Uçhisar.

The new urban settlement of Göreme, built among the ancient tufa pinnacles.

of constructions and lodgings built into the rock-face in ancient times and recently, since they are still in use. Inside them countless niches have been carved out for birds who, by nesting there, form layers of guano which is then collected and used as fertilizer.

A deep gorge opens up near Uçhisar; originally a confluence of waterways, a canyon heads in the direction of Ak Vadi. The plateau eroded by the rivers features a cleft where the vegetation ceases to grow, giving way to white, curved slopes. The very name of the crags has given the valley its name: "snow white"; at the bottom of the steep slopes, the gorge of the river bed becomes a chasm and the vertical walls are marked horizontally by various degrees of erosion.

Continuing along the road from Uçhisar and heading northwards one arrives in **Avçilar**, situated near the turn-offs to Çavusin and Zelve in the north and Göreme in the east.

Avçilar also dates back to ancient times; evidence of this lies in the tomb, attributed to the Roman era, whose half-crumbling facade rises up near the village on a rock. In fact it is a type of rock tomb with its facade carved out of the rocky mass and honeycombed rooms. Originally the facade was designed as a sort of temple pronaos, embellished by a triangular gable; below it two moldings imitate the space of the trabeation, supported by two columns crowned with simplified Doric capitals.

GÖREME

The Göreme area has been occupied since the dawn of history; more recently it was occupied by Christians who, under the threat of Muslim attacks, moved to this area where geological conditions made it easier to hide. In fact, the oldest churches in the area — very few of which are still standing — date back to the 7th century. Christians and communities of monks turned the area into a place of refuge and refreshment, setting up their hide-outs inside the tufa pinnacles, which were easily camouflaged and defended. With the exception of the Iconoclastic period (between 715 and 843) when the churches only tolerated abstract, symbolic decorations, painting came into its own here, leading to a Cappadocian style. The animals depicted each represented something: the fish (the letters of the Greek word for form the acrostic "Jesus Christ, Son of God, the Saviour") symbolizes Christ himself, while the dove has always been the symbol of peace and the Holy Spirit. Deer symbolize the soul and peacocks the resurrection whereas the symbolical tradi-

tions of other animals go far back in time: the cock — which represented the day, vitality and light and, in the wider sense, goodness to the Greeks — and the palm, direct oriental evolution of the tree of life and portrayal of vital energy and eternity.

Some rock structures in the area were used for burial purposes: one of the most evocative examples is to be found upon one's arrival in Göreme, where a rock pinnacle contains a mortuary chapel embellished by a small facade. The interior features a square room with a bench running along to a lunette apse; in the floor — and at a later stage also in the benched part — graves were hewn; they were then covered by fitted slabs.

The Göreme area also includes the **El Nazar valley** where the fairy chimneys house rock complexes, like the "Church of the Madonna"; the nearby valley of Kiliçlar Vadisi contains another church called "Church of Kiliçlar", which, despite its lack of frescoes, boasts fine four-columned architecture.

The Girls Monastery in the open-air rock museum of Göreme.

CAVE CHURCHES OF GÖREME

In the valley of Göreme stands an Open-Air Museum which used to house a religious community. Numerous churches make up a large monastic complex, all hewn out of the cliffs and crags. The promoter of the community was St Basil — Bishop of Caesarea (Kayseri) — who wanted to break away from the tendency at the time towards rather large communities or individual hermitages.

Local tradition has it that there were as many as 365 churches, one for each day of the year, of which about thirty are open to the public. All churches still standing in Göreme were built after about 850 A.D. and decorated up to the 11th century with frescoes which,

despite their Byzantine influence, have extremely simple lines.

Architectural features were enhanced by paintings by professional artists financed by locals.

Various inscriptions — sometimes accompanied by portraits — bear the name of the artist and his financers; accurate historic and iconographic research have ascertained that benefactors were usually country squires who sometimes formed trusts to carry out costly works of art.

It is the very impermeability of tufa, apart from the constant temperature of the rooms, that has kept the colours alive after so many centuries.

The north wall of the Tokali Kilise,
and the Pantocrator in the central dome
of the Elmali Kilise.

The exterior of the Karanlik Kilise and the Crucifixion.

KARANLIK KILISE

The so-called Karanlik Kilise, or "Dark Church" was in fact a real monastic complex. Like other monastic retreats in Göreme, the Dark Church was also built during the 11th century, financed by at least four benefactors portrayed in its frescoes. Unfortunately, part of its narthex collapsed, leaving it open to the sky. The church's name is fully justified: in fact, a small oculus looking out on the narthex is the only source of light. However, it was this protection against the light and changes in humidity that has preserved the fine frescoes of Karanlik Kilise over the centuries. The scenes depicted in the church represent episodes from the *New Testament*, on a blue background made of lapislazuli; the most outstanding panels portray *Christ Almighty* on the main dome, the *Nativity*, the *Baptism*, the *Last Supper*, *Christ's Betrayal*, the *Crucifixion* and pictures of the various *Saints* and *Evangelists*.

In the Paşabag area small vineyards grow among the fairy chimneys.

THE FAIRY CHIMNEYS

Near Zelve, in the Paşabag area, one can admire in a valley the so-called "fairy chimneys", or "peri baca-si" in the local dialect. The valley is also known as the Valley of Monks due to the hermitages inside the tufa pinnacles.

What makes the valley exceedingly strange is the unusual shape of the stone formations; their chimney-pot shape led to the ancient legend that they were inhabited by fairies capable of casting all sorts of spells. The geological history of the fairy chimneys dates back many centuries: as we all know, the region is of volcanic origin and therefore consists of lithic types of varying quality and hardness. The Paşabag area, like most of the rest of the area, consists mainly of tufa rock, which, however is associated with harder types of basaltic rocks, recognisable in the "crown" of the chimneys. The combined action of various erosive

agents wore away the surface layer of the hard, dark rock, exposing the highly friable underlying tufa. Therefore all that remains of the surface layer nowadays, is the "hat" of the pinnacles; beneath them, a clear, almost horizontal line indicates the lower margin of the original lithic fault. The blocks that have remained isolated by erosion — especially of rain water — have since been split vertically, transforming them into pinnacles joined to one another or into groups of pinnacles.

The work of nature has been accompanied by the work of man: many pinnacles have been hewn out for hermitages and dwelling-places. The most unusual one is the chimney along the road featuring a hat at the top of a sort of natural column; inside was a chapel and other rooms were hewn out of the adjacent "hatless" needles.

Panorama of Zelve, and a rock-hewn church.

ZELVE

Zelve, like the rest of the Cappadocian region, is of volcanic origin. The volcano of Monte Argaeus ("Erciyeş Dağ" in the local dialect) is still active; 3,917 meters high, it dominates the whole area and can be seen at a distance. As in the case of other unusually-shaped rock formations, the different compositions of the rocks and their resulting hardness (tufas, basalts) has enabled the various agents to mold the region in surrealistic ways.

The village was built in the erosion furrows and into the rock-face, hewing out the tufa rock and sometimes exploiting large openings eroded by water. In these huge caves, entrances were dug to the deepest homes or, more recently, the small buildings in masonry. The local community — first Christian and then Muslim —

was numerous and has left traces of its unusual way of tunnelling through the bowels of the earth to construct a wide range of facilities; a church, water storage points, a mill, a flat-roofed room with benches in which a stone disc with a handle acted as a grindstone, rotating inside a drum cut out of the rock. Among the most important constructions are some churches which are the oldest examples of architecture and religious painting in the region.

The **Üzümlü Kilise**, or Church with the Grapes, is named after bunches of grapes schematically depicted on a whitish background in between vine-leaves. It is interesting to note the way the bunch has been reduced graphically to a rough, dark triangle without outlining the individual grapes. Already a religious symbol for

Greek Dionysian rituals and for other previous Eastern religions, according to the Christian religion, the vine represents Christ himself.

When Zelve was taken over by Muslims, it also contained a mosque hewn out of the rock. These cave houses were inhabited until 1950, when the progressive geological degradation of the mass and continuous excavations to create new rooms — despite curtain walls — led to dangerous rockfalls in the troglodyte dwellings. At this stage, the community was evacuated to the modern part of Zelve, or Yeni Zelve.

The Üzümlü Kilise, or Church of the Grapes, with the fresco which gives the church its name and the double-naved interior.

Avanos is famous for its terracottas. Typical vases on display in front of the potters' shops.

AVANOS

The town of Avanos dates back to the Bronze Age, as can be seen from the burial tumulus of Toprakli. On the other hand, its terrain is watered by the 1355 kilometer-long Kizilirmak River, the longest river in Turkey. This river was known to the Hittites as Marassantiya, while in the Classic Age it was known as Halys; its current name means "red river", due to the color of its waters in this section of the river.

The very name of Avanos, which comes from the Latin "Venasa", refers to the banks of ferrous minerals which color the silt, collected in quarries and refined in order to obtain the raw material for pottery. In fact, pottery is one of the main activities in the center; in one of the town squares, a monument recalls various local activities such as vine-growing and weaving but especially, pottery. Many streets are flanked by small potter's workshops where potters, seated in front of simple pedal turn-tables flanked by characteristic terracotta basins, make all kinds of pots. They are most famous for their highly lustrous pottery, whose shiny red surface is decorated with vegetable and geometric designs.

Similar motifs appear on carpets, which, in Avanos as in other areas in the region, is a traditional activity. Carpets are not only produced in workshops, but countless women weave them at home, utilizing silk and wool patiently knotted on wooden looms. These products often appear on the streets of the town, flanked by old buildings in blocks of tufa and by houses with Muslim architecture, including a loggia terrace on the front.

VALLEY OF SOĞANLI

A complex of religious buildings dug into the tufa, similar to the Open-Air Museum in Göreme, stands in **Soğanli**, 25 kilometers from Derinkuyu, an area of pigeon-lofts: in fact, pigeon-lofts were installed in churches which had been abandoned a long time beforehand. Their progressive emptying and restoration has enabled many Christian temples on the banks of the village stream to be brought back to their former glory. The churches, which probably date back to the 9th century onwards, feature simple plans and ornate paintings in bright colors like blue, green, red and black on a beige background. Paintings follow the usual themes of Christ, saints, religious symbols and animals, but certain panels also contain outlandish figures, perhaps connected to preexisting cults.

Among the numerous noteworthy churches is the **Church with the Beast**, named after a wild animal next to St John in a fresco. Of the two rooms, one has an altar and wall burial niches, whereas the other communicating room is built according to a simple square plan.

The **Kubbeli Kilise**, or Church with a dome, in fact, consists of two churches on different stories. The interior of the area of worship, which is reached through three portals, has benches and is divided into three aisles by two rows of pillars and pilaster strips; the side aisles, like the nave, lead to curved apsidioles with altars.

However, the top floor has a far more complex plan consisting of two long, parallel, intercommunicating rooms, each of which has a narthex. The right-hand chapel has a small apse with an altar and a narthex with a dome; the other chapel has its altar against the back wall and a square narthex, which overlooks not only its church but the one next door, a vestibule and an inside room.

In fact the **Church of St Barbara** also comprises two adjacent churches. Despite its bad state of repair and damage to the paintings, it can be deduced that the two parallel rooms were virtually the same but with different proportions. In the remains of frescoes, the figure of a saint has been roughly indicated as St Barbara, thus giving the complex its name.

The **Karabaş Kilise** or Church with the Black Heads owes its name to the images of the saints whose faces have been blackened by deterioration and oxidation. Crumbling in parts, it consists of several communicating rooms each with its own altar (except for the one in the middle).

Characteristic pigeon-lofts in the Soğanli Valley. The lofts are ringed in white to attract the attention of the birds who make their nests there.

DERINKUYU AND KAYMAKLI

One of the most surprising complexes in the region is **Derinkuyu**, a huge underground city. Below the nineteenth century church are seven stories of rooms, corridors, kitchens, a conference room, cemeteries and churches which were hewn out in time until they covered, on communicating floors, an area of 4 square kilometers, capable of accommodating 20,000 inhabitants. Air shafts, consisting of vertical wells connected to water-tanks, are quite a feat.

About **Kaymakli** one could quite rightly say that the town has been inhabited since the 5th century B.C. The complex comprises several floors, sometimes connected by steep air shafts terminating in cisterns. The entrances were closed by an ingenious blocking system: an enormous stone wheel, similar to a grindstone, was usually kept in a niche, from where it could easily be rolled towards the passage, isolating it completely. A central hole in the stone wheel enabled it to be removed with a pivot and its prop allowed the troglodyte to shore up the door.

The facility with which the soft stone was worked induced them to carve out of the rock furniture which they would otherwise have extracted from wood: cupboards, tables, beds and shelves. Nowadays the underground village is equipped with electric lighting facilitating tours.

Two views of the underground cities of Derinkuyu and Kaymakli.

The Seljuk citadel dominates the city of Nevşehir.

NEVŞEHIR

Nowadays Nevşehir, capital of a large area, looks like one of the typical modern towns in Anatolia. The site on which it now stands, over one thousand meters high, was occupied in ancient times: races of the Neolithic Age have been documented through the tumulus of Iğdeli Çeşme and other obsidian finds. The town was probably refounded during the Hittite era because it is near to Kizilirmark. Having become an important town, it was occupied by Aegeans towards the 12th century B.C. and by Cimmerians towards the 8th century B.C., passing under the Assyrians between 680 and 610 B.C., then under the Medes until 550 and under the Persians until 332 B.C. After the Hellenistic age, Nevşehir was occupied by the Romans from 17 A.D., who then left it to Byzantium from 395; having then passed under various dominions (of the Ilhanlilars, the Eretnas and the Karamangullaris), it was annexed to the Ottoman Empire in 1446.

Very little evidence remains of its past rulers: the fortress, which overlooks the modern town, dates back to the Byzantine era. The Seljuk and Ottoman restorations made it into a pentagonal fortress with four cylindrical towers and two entrances; the wall, which partly skirts the rocky crags, is crenellated.

Lower down is a large Islamic religious complex: the mosque of Ibrahim Paşa also known as the Mosque with the Leads on account of the lead tiles on the roof. Damat Ibrahim Paşa was the local Grand Vizier at the beginning of the eighth century who commissioned the mosque with its outbuildings, which were completed eight years later. The architect who designed it was inspired by mosques in the capital, placing near the entrance a garden with a fountain covered by a dome on columns that precedes the domed portico. The interior with spectacular decorated vaults features a precious enamelled altar with a passage from the Koran.

The local benefactor of this mosque has been commemorated with a recently built statue in the central square behind the religious complex. It portrays Dama Ibrahim Paşa in his Vizier's uniform and high headdress. He also had part of the hostel, which now serves as the local museum, built. The rooms, inaugurated in 1967, house a series of documents on local history, including hand-written, illuminated codexes; the archaeological section — with its crockery, weapons, clothes and every day utensils — and the ethnographical section — exhibiting local traditional arts and crafts — are of particular interest.

THE VALLEY OF IHLARA

The countryside in the valley of Ihlara is different from the rest of Cappadocia: in fact, a river-bed has opened a deep canyon in the rocky tableland; only in the bottom of this steep valley does vegetation manage to grow.

The valley of Ihlara has another entire complex of churches in a steep, picturesque valley. Dating back as far as the 4th century, their 9th- century frescoes are inspired by Syrian art which was simpler and made use of only a few colors (various shades of red on a white background).

As for the 11th century, more colors were used and the Syrian-Egyptian style was influenced by Byzantine art and religious mosaics of major churches at the time. Starting from the south, after the Kuzey Ambar Kilise, we encounter the **Kokar Kilise** (literally translated, it means the church that smells) dating back to the 9th century, and distinguished by its light green on grey frescoes and burial chambers. Having passed the Parenli Seki Kilise, one comes across the **Ağaç Alti Kilise**, or the church under the trees; in fact, the valley is dotted with tall trees whose growth is encouraged by the stream and milder climate. Nearby stands the **Sümbüllü Kilise**, or church of the hyacinths, whose facade is embellished with arched niches.

On the opposite side, near the Karanlik Kaya Kilise or Dark Church stands the **Ylanli Kilise** or Church with Snakes, named after the fresco with snakes attacking four sinners.

Another noteworthy church is the **Eğritaş Kilise**, used as a funeral chapel whose frescoes portray scenes from the *Life of Christ and Mary*. Near the village of Belisirma stands the cross-shaped **Ala Kilise**, with its crumbling domes.

A stone's throw away is the **Bakattin Samakiliği Kilise**, whose vaulted, single-columned interior is decorated with valuable frescoes.

Another church of interest in the neighborhood is the **Kirm Damalti Kilise**, also known as the Church of St George. On the opposite side of Melendiz is the cross-shaped **Direkli Kilise**, whose central dome supported by four columns and walls are decorated with frescoes, probably dating back to the 11th-12th centuries.

The course of the Melendiz has excavated the deep canyon which forms the valley of Ihlara.

A view of modern Kayseri, with the monument to Atatürk.

The Döner Kümbet, or "rotating mausoleum", 13th century.

KAYSERI

This large city in Cappadocia stands over 1000 m. above sea level, at the center of a territory dominated by the perennial snows on the peak of Erciyas Daği (3916 m.). In ancient times this mountain was known as Mount Argaeus and was an active volcano. Now inactive, one of the liveliest and best known ski resorts in Turkey is situated on its slopes.

The origins of the city of Kayseri are ancient and it was already known in pre-Roman times. The Emperor Tiberias called it *Caesarea* and as the chief city in Cappadocia its role as an administrative center was soon affirmed.

Modern Kayseri is an active pulsating city in keeping with the times, in which the often strident contrasts between the old and the new frequently come to the fore. Its economic structure, while not repudiating the traditional craft industries which furnish fine carpets and splendid examples of the goldsmith's art, is taking on marked industrial characteristics.

The remains of the ancient **Citadel**, built by the Byzantines and consolidated by the Seljuks, are represented by a circuit of walls with towers, built in lava stone. An interesting *Bedesten*, blanket market, takes place around this fortified structure and the skilful local craftsmen here display their wares.

Near the **Honat Hatum Camii** (13th cent.), distinguished for its finely executed decor, is a particularly interesting architectural complex which consists of a *madrasah* and an octagonal *türbeh* which contains some good sarcophaguses. The ensemble was erected by the princess Mapheri, wife of the sovereign Alaeddin Keykubat.

The **Ulu Camii**, or *Great Mosque*, dates to the first half of the 14th century and has a particularly suggestive interior enriched by magnificent hand-made carpets.

Of the numerous local mausoleums mention must be made of the **Döner Kümbet**, (13th cent.) of particular note for its interesting architectural and ornamental features, the **Sirçalı Kümbet** and the ancient **Kasbek Kümbet**, datable to the second half of the 13th century. Also worthwhile mentioning are the remains of a *hypogeum* from the Roman period and the **Cifte Medrese**, where there was a school of anatomy in the Middle Ages.

*The Selimiye Camii in the foreground, and on the left
the Mausoleum of Mevlâna.*

KONYA

Over 1000 m. above sea level, this important city in central southern Turkey is situated at the lower edge of the vast Anatolian highlands, with the Taurus mountain chain in the distance. Konya is one of the major tourist attractions in Turkey in virtue of the testimony of the past in which the history, culture, and architecture of this ancient city become one.

The site where modern Konya stands has been inhabited from the most distant times; various archaeological finds have even pushed the dates of the city back to 7000 B.C. although more prudent estimates do not confirm the existence of human settlements before the third millennium B.C. An incontestable fact, however, is that Konya was one of the subject cities of the vast Hittite realm, even if it also developed substantially under the Phrygians. The Romans called it *Iconium*, a name by which it was generally known in the past. In part, the Roman place name explains its present denomination, apparently tied to an "icon", the story of which is however rooted in myth. In the first century A.D. the city witnessed the apostolate of saints Paul and Barnaba who played an important role in the evangelization of this area. In the first half of the 3rd century, a council was held in Konya, while the early

Middle Ages witnessed the usual comings and goings of various peoples. Capital of the Seljuk sultans (11th cent.) it was then assimilated to the Ottoman empire by Mehmet II (15th cent.) . Events centered in Konya acquired a particular dimension from the first half of the 13th century on, when it was chosen as dwelling place by Ğelâleddîn Rûmî, who passed into history as *Mevlâna*. Poet and philosopher, he was the founder of the mystic-religious sect of the *Whirling Dervishes* which still today constitutes one of the most qualified expressions of the traditions and folklore of Turkey, as well as one of the most intimate manifestations of the profound piety and mysticism of the Turks rooted in folk culture. The celebrations in honor of Mevlâna held yearly in December are truly unforgettable. The tourists can then watch the complex rituals of the Dervish dancers who wear traditional costumes and their unusual hats.

The **Monastery-Mausoleum of Mevlâna** is heralded by the superb conical fluted dome of an intense turquoise which stands out against the sky. The setting of this architectural jewel consists of other domes and minarets. This complex of buildings is at the head of the list of sites visited by the tourist. Particularly worthy of note is the *türbeh* (13th cent.) with the sarcophagus of Ḡelâleddîn Rûmî and his close relatives, and the other rooms in the monastery which have been transformed into a Dervish museum. Outstanding, among the innumerable objects, are the Manuscripts of the *Mesnevi* (a mystic epic poem by Mevlâna) and of the *Divan El Kebir*.

The **Alaeddin Camii** takes its name from the sovereign under whom it was terminated in the first half of the 13th century. Stylistically of great interest, it offers for contemplation the splendid *mihrab* and *mimbar*, numbered among the masterpieces of 12th-century wood carving. Note also the wooden roof of the hall used for worship, supported by numerous columns with fine capitals, and the mausoleum (12th cent.) situated in the courtyard.

The objects belonging to the local *Museum of Wood and Stone Sculpture* can be seen in the **Ince Minareli Medrese** with its charming finely ornamented portal and the minaret lopped off by a bolt of lighting.

The **Karatay Medrese**, once founded as a Koran school (13th cent.), is decorated with an elegant doorway and is now a museum. It houses the interesting collections that are part of the *Ceramic Museum*, including exquisitely made examples of the Seljuk potter's craft. Other sites of interest in the city are the **Sirçali Museum**, once a school of canonic law (13th cent.), now housing sarcophaguses and funerary monuments of the Seljuk, Karaman and Ottoman periods, the **Museum of Turkish-Islamic Art**, the modern **Atatürk Museum**, and the interesting collections of the **Archaeological Museum**, found in the course of excavations in the city and immediate vicinity.

The lovely Türbeh of the mausoleum of Mevlâna, with its intense green color that can be seen from anywhere in the city.

The famous ''Whirling Dervishes'': the right hand is raised in prayer the left points towards the ground, the whirling movement of the dance symbolizes the rotation of the universe around God.

The vestiges of the sacred precinct (temenos) of Athena.

The marble columns of the Temple of Trajan, in Corinthian style.

BERGAMA

Basically Bergama is a modern city with the characteristic features of a typical Turkish village. Its fame and exceptional fascination for the tourist derive from the presence in the vicinity of the vestiges of ancient *Pergamum* (Greek, Pergamon), one of the most famous cities in the Ancient World. The site where the ancient settlements developed is situated in a fertile plain irrigated by the waters of the river Bergama Cayl (the ancient *Selinus*) and of the rivers Kestel and Bakır. Even though historical mention of Pergamon has not been ascertained prior to the 4th century B.C., the opinion generally held is that the origins of the city are by far earlier. Various archaeological finds datable to the Stone Age testify to the antiquity of the first human settlements. The history of what then became one of the most flourishing Hellenistic cities began with the dismemberment of the immense Persian empire, after the death of Alexander the Great. Lysimachos, who received the western part of Anatolia, chose the impervious site of Pergamon as the hiding place for a considerable treasure. Philetairos, a faithful follower, succeeded in preserving the integrity of the treasure and the possession of the city when Lysimachos died, despite attempts on the part of Antiochus I. His grandson Eumenes I proclaimed the independence of the new realm of Pergamon (3rd cent. B.C.), which with his successors, in particular Eumenes II, shone in the fields of economy, the arts, the sciences and culture. With the death of Attalus II, in 133 B.C., the Kingdom of Pergamon, lacking natural heirs, was pacifically

*The colonnade of the north gallery of the Aesculapium,
or Temple of Aesculapius, built in the 2nd century A.D.*

taken over by the Roman Senate which thus reaped the harvest of old agreements and alliances. Under the Capitoline standard the city enjoyed a great new period of development which manifested itself in the construction of splendid buildings and in the restoration of various monuments of the past. Later Marc Antony presented Cleopatra with the city's rich library, the books of which, of incalculable value, were eventually destroyed in a fire in Egypt. The decadance of Pergamon, now known as Pergamum, followed the disintegration of the Roman empire step by step. Seat of a diocese in the Christian period, it was surrounded by new city walls by the Byzantines who reused material of Hellenistic and Roman provenance in its construction. After 716 Pergamum was taken over by the Arabs, and passed under the control of the Turks in the first half of the 14th century.

The history of the archaeological excavations began in the second half of the 19th century when the archaeologists C. Humann, A. Conze and R. Bohn brought to light the upper portion of the city. Later excavations, conducted between 1900 and 1913 by W. Dörpfeld, H.

The remains of the broad road that led to the acropolis.

Hepding and P. Schatzmann, uncovered the lower levels. Work undertaken by T. Wiegand between 1927 and 1936 hoped to find a precise identification for some of the illustrious buildings of the past. The most recent excavations began in 1957 and were directed by E. Boehringer with excellent results, while further investigation is in course to restore in their entirety all that remains of the monuments and artistic treasures of the past.

The vestiges of numerous private and public buildings and temples have been found along the vast extension of the **Acropolis**, which occupies the highest part of the city. This is where the famous **Library** built in the time of Eumenes II (2nd cent. B.C.) once stood. It soon became famous throughout the Ancient World for its wealth of volumes, estimated at over 200,000, and was long a rival of the equally famous Library of Alexandria in Egypt. The enormous *statue of Athena*, now in the Pergamon Museum in Berlin, once stood in the Library.

The ruins of the **Temple of Trajan**, built to honor the cult of the deified Trajan, lie on a terrace that

Remains of the stoa which was part of the
Aesculapium, in Doric style.

dominates the remains of the library. It was a Corinthian temple, with a row of six columns on the short sides and nine on the long sides. The remains of two statues dedicated to Trajan and to his successor Hadrian, under whom the construction of the temple was terminated between 117 and 118 A.D., were also found here.

The vestiges of the majestic *Temple of Athena* have been shifted to right over the theatre. The Propylaeum of the temple with its elegant double columned portico has been faithfully rebuilt in the Berlin Museum. The temple, originally decorated with fine reliefs, was erected in the 3rd century B.C., in line with the architectural canons of the Doric order and had six columns on the short sides and ten on the longer ones.

The nearby **Theatre** was probably built in the Hellenistic period during the reign of Eumenes II (2nd cent. B.C.) although some hypotheses date it as far back as the 4th century B.C. The imposing structure is enumerated among the most scenographic in antiquity. The steep cavea, set against the slope of the hill, was divided into six sectors in its upper part and seven below, and had an audience capacity of 10,000 with perfect acoustics. Not far from the theatre is the **Temple of Dionysios**, built in the 2nd century B.C. and restored in the imperial age by Caracalla, after the original building had been gutted by fire.

Among the other outstanding elements on the acropolis mention must be made of the scanty traces of what remains of the **Altar of Zeus**. Built to celebrate the victory over the Galatians during the reign of Eumenes II (2nd cent. B.C.) it has been moved and faithfully rebuilt in Berlin, one of the highlights of the Pergamon Museum. The fine frieze depicting episodes of the *Gigantomachy*, and counted among the greatest masterpieces of the Pergamene sculptor's art, was also taken to Berlin together with the structures of the altar.

The ruins of another **Hellenistic temple** dedicated to the cult of **Hera** can also be seen in the vicinity. Built under Attalos I, at the turn of the 3rd century B.C., the obvious restorations date to Roman times. Other buildings that lie immediately below the acropolis include various constructions used as a gymnasium and for baths.

At the foot of the slope of the acropolis, right where

The ruins of the imposing Altar of Zeus and the remains of a Roman statue.

the river Bergama Cayl flows, stand the imposing vestiges of the so-called **Red Court** or **Red Basilica**, originally a Serapeion built under Hadrian (2nd cent. A.D.). The curious name derives from the intense color of the bricks with which it was built. Signs of later transformation, in the Byzantine period, into a basilica can still be seen. Two subterranean galleries consented the outflow of the waters of the ancient Selinus. In the environs, a Roman bridge with three arches can be identified.

The so-called *Sacred Way*, once flanked by columns, leads to what remains of the **Aesculapium**, without doubt the best-known temple of ancient Pergamon. The temple already existed in pre-Roman times and was consecrated in honor of Aesculapius, god of medicine. All that is left of this imposing complex in which healing and worship went hand in hand, are the ruins of the *Propyleia* erected in the 2nd century A.D., a few re-erected columns and traces of the library, a circular temple originally covered with a dome, as well as rooms destined for baths. The annexed *Theatre* held up to 3,500 spectators and is still used for summer spectacles.

View from above of Izmir, known also in Europe as Smyrna.

IZMIR

This large and populous city (third largest in population after Istanbul and Ankara) overlooking the Aegean coast is the heir to the ancient *Smyrna*. In appearance it is basically modern, the result, in great part, of the fire which destroyed most of the city in 1922. An active port of call for shipping, second in importance only to that of Istanbul, it is considered an ideal point of departure for excursions in a surrounding territory that has much to offer. One of the most characteristic features of Izmir is its felicitous geographical site, at the foot of the hill on which the fortress of Kadifekale stands, facing out on an enchanting bay, with a natural backdrop of high mountains which in antiquity were a valid bulwark against threatened aggressions from outside.

Archaeological investigation carried out between the 1940s and 50s and begun again in the middle of the 60s has born out the hypothesis that the first forms of settlement on the soil of Smyrna were datable to the 3rd millennium B.C. and could be located in what is known today as Bayraklı. Scholars think the original nucleus of the city was coeval with the first levels of the city of Troy and that Smyrna adopted some of the cultural and religious models of Hittite civilization. Potsherds also document the presence of a Hellenic settlement dating to the 10th century B.C. Devastated by the Lydians around the 7th century B.C., the city was rebuilt in the second half of the 4th century B.C., under the auspices of Alexander the Great. Successively part of the Realm of Pergamon, it was eventually included in the territories controlled by Rome and was embellished with new majestic buildings. In 178 A.D. Smyrna was razed to the ground by an earthquake and reconstruction was begun with the effective good

Nothing is more relaxing than a fine walk along the sea-front promenade of Izmir.

The Kanak Camii.

offices of Marcus Aurelius. The Arab raids in the 7th century marked the beginning of its decadence. Taken over by the Seljuks (11th cent.) its vicissitudes varied at the time of the Crusades and it was permanently taken over by the Ottoman dynasty in the 15th century. A flourishing commercial center, it attracted European traders over a long period of time, survived repeated catastrophic earthquakes which struck once more in the 17th and 18th centuries. At the end of World War I Smyrna was entrusted to Greek control, from which it was released by the victorious progression of the struggle for national liberation under Atatürk.

The scanty remains of the Agora however attest to the city's great past; apparently it was built during the Hellenistic period, even if what is to be seen today certainly dates to a reconstruction promoted by Faustina,

The Clock Tower, built in 1901 in Moorish style, is 25 meters high.

A beautiful view of Çeşme Kale.

Marcus Aurelius' wife, right after the devastating earthquake of 178 A.D. Various statues of the Roman period are particularly interesting. Partially mutilated, they represent *Neptune*, *Ceres* and *Diana*.

Another element of particular interest to the tourist is the so-called **Kadifekale**. This fortress, whose name is the equivalent in English of "velvet fortress", dominates the city from what in antiquity was known as *Mount Pagus*. Its appearance today is that of a structure readapted in Byzantine times even if its origins doubtless go back to before the period of Roman colonization.

The **Archaeological Museums** of the city contain many interesting finds, which came to light in the course of excavations in various archaeological zones of western Anatolia. Of particular note is a headless statue of a woman from Erythrai, and dating to the 6th century B.C. Other documentation includes examples of archaic sculpture (second half of the 6th cent. B.C.), expressions of Hellenistic art, Roman and Byzantine sculpture, as well as good example of sculpture from Ephesus (2nd cent. A.D.).

In the list of other tourist attractions in Izmir, mention should be made of the **Kültür Parki**, seat of the annual international fair, the **Bazaar**, which displays the characteristic craft objects, the **Hisar** and **Kemeraltı Mosques** (16th cent.), the caravanserai of **Kizlarağasi** and the so-called **Clock Tower**, with its fine architectural details, situated near the *Yahli Camii* (18th cent.).

The fine architecture of the Gymnasium of Sardis.

SARDIS

The importance of Sardis in history rests on the fact that i t was the capital of the ancient kingdom of Lydia. If the figures of some of its kings such as the mythical Croesus and Gige are in great part based on myth, it is certain that the Lydians were famous for their capacities in the fields of trade and economics. After being conquered by Alexander the Great (4th cent. B.C.), Sardis gradually became more and more Hellenistic. In the 2nd century B.C. the city passed under the control of the sovereigns of Pergamon and was then incorporated into the Roman empire. It was already an important religious center in the Byzantine period, and was taken over by the Turks in the 14th century.

At the center of the acropolis, from which come potsherds dating to the 7th century B.C., can be seen the remains of structures of the Byzantine period. The so-called *Castle of Antiochus III* is a towered structure of the Hellenistic period between 223 and 187 B.C. The most significant remains have been shifted to a street that was originally (4th cent.) lined with columns. Of

note are the vestiges of a **Gymnasium** of the Imperial age (3rd cent.) with a columned two-story facade. An inscription mentions Caracalla, his brother Geta and their mother Julia Domna, as well as the date in which work came to an end (211 A.D.).

In the vicinity is a coeval **Synagogue** in which fine paintings and frescoes of the 4th century and noteworthy mosaic pavements have been uncovered. The other vestiges of the past worthy of mention include the **Baths**, a **Theatre** of the 3rd century B.C., a Hellenistic **Cemetery**, and the so-called **House of Bronzes** (6th cent. A.D.) with a considerable number of bronzes of the Byzantine period.

The ruins of the **Temple of Artemis** are fairly well preserved. Originally built during the reign of Lydia, it was rebuilt in Hellenistic times and in the Roman period, when it was dedicated to the cult of the emperor Antoninus Pius. In the 5th century A.D. the rear part of the building was restructured to house the Christian cult.

Detail of the Odeion: even though it was meant for Senate meetings, theater spectacles were also often held here.

EPHESUS

The foundation of Ephesus by colonists unquestionably of Hellenic stock took place between the 16th and 11th centuries B.C. In the 7th century the city and its greatest symbol, the Artemision, were totally destroyed by the Cimmerian hordes. Rebuilt by Croesus, king of the Lydians, it was subjugated by the Persian king Cyrus in the middle of the 6th century. After varying vicissitudes, Ephesos pacifically and painlessy passed to the Romans. Evidence of the importance Ephesus had in the Roman world are the visits paid by such illustrious figures as Brutus, Cassius, Antony, and Cicero himself. In the Augustan age it was a real Asian capital. The city grew and soon became an active commercial center, headquarters of the Roman governor and one of the first five cities of the Empire. Subsequently the preaching of the apostle John (buried here in St. John's church) and a tradition according to which the Madonna chose it as her residence after the Crucifixion, turned Ephesus into one of the places that distinguished itself in the history of Christian thought. Its decline began in the second half of the 3rd century when it was conquered and sacked by the Goths. In 431 the Third Ecumenical Council was held here. During the long dark centuries of the Middle Ages it was little more than a village, subject to continuous raids by the Arabs and pirates. After the early years of Ottoman rule, it fell into complete oblivion. Abandoned and deserted, all trace of it almost disappeared until 1869 when the first of the archaeological excavations which were to restore to the world the ancient and unforgotten beauty of the city was undertaken.

Doric columns with Corinthian capitals, part of the Basilica.

Ruins of the Prytaneion: an inscription and a pedestal depicting Hermes.

ODEION

This semi-circular structure, known also as the Small Theatre, is set on the slopes of the hills to the north of the Agora. An inscription of 150 A.D. attributes its foundation to a certain Publius Vedius Antonius, who conceived it as a *bouleuterion* or meeting place for the Senate. In reality, the original structure was covered over, and with a capacity of 1,400 seated spectators, it alternatively served as bouleuterion and as a small theatre. The architectural design partially follows this classic of analogous models of antiquity; the *auditorium* with double rows, semi-circular in form, is divided into four main wedges by stairs separated from the passageways; while the unusual structure of the proscenium clearly denotes the intention of its builders who wanted the most suitable building for housing the meetings of the Senate, rather than theatrical performances.

The Street of the Curetes — a view towards the Library of Celsus, and a sculpture along the way.

AGORA

The ruins which can be seen at present refer to a Roman building of the Imperial Age (1st century A.D.), probably finished off in the time of Augustus and Claudius. The Agora, which received its final accomodation under Theodosius (4th century), was decorated with a double colonnade (*stoa*) where commercial activities were carried on. A fulcrum of mercantile activities, it was frequented by merchants coming from every corner of the Empire; it also entertained the slave market, and was the hub for civil and religious festivities.

To the north of the Agora rise the cropped stones of the columns of the **Basilica** which was erected during the Augustan era. Several columns which have survived are indicative of an unmistakable Doric vestige, while the coping of the capital is obviously Corinthian in its imprint.

PRYTANEION

Its function in antiquity was comparable to that of our town hall: in addition to public functions, it housed important events, receptions and banquets. In the annexed *Temple of Hestia Boulaia* there burned perennially the sacred fire which the Pritanei — the priests who attended to the citizens' worship and to the sacrificial practice — had to feed.

Its construction can be dated with certainty to the 3rd century B.C.

STREET OF THE CURETES

This street which goes up the slope between the *Library of Celsius* and the *Gate of Heracles* is certainly the most charming Ephesian thouroughfare in the center of the ancient city. It attained its splendour at the time of restoration of the road which, towards the middle of the 4th century, had been ramshackle and made unusable by a violent and ruinous earthquake. Its inclusion in a countryside and environment which boasts elements of extreme fascination and appeal, harmonizes — by means of the precious structure of marble and stone pavements — with the remains of antiquity that surround it, in a remarkable picture punctuated by columns, stumps of stone pedestals, podiums, ornamented capitals, friezes, inscriptions, statues and traces of buildings for commercial use and for use as habitations. In this vast profusion of antique ruins, often specially carried from other areas of the city, stand out covered columned galleries whose pavements are made precious by refined mosaics. The empty pedestals, which in great numbers face the group of columns, were once surmounted by statues: a great many of them bear several interesting engraved epigraphs. Many of the statues were transferred to the Museum.

The name of the street refers to mythological characters who in a later epoch gave name to the cast of priests of the Curetes. The latter devoted themselves initially to the services which were celebrated in the Artemision but, subsequently, they found a place also inside the Prytaneion. Numerous inscriptions on their role can be found in different parts of the city, even if the citations of great prominence are to be found in the Prytaneion. It is known that their number — initially composed of six units — was later raised to nine.

Another detail of architecture along the Street of the Curetes.

Hadrian's Temple with the houses on the hill in the background.

A detail of Hadrian's Temple: note the bust of Tyche on the arch and the Medusa in the semicircular lunette.

TEMPLE OF HADRIAN

An inscription sculpted into the architrave of the temple gives testimony to its construction around 138 A.D. by the hand of a certain P. Quintilius, who dedicated it to Emperor Hadrian. Facing the monumental pronaos also arose the pedestals of four statues which formerly decorated the building. When reading the inscriptions sculpted on each of them, we learn that the carved figures depicted Diocletian, Maximian, Constantius Clorus and Galerius.

The temple is markedly Corinthian, and is distinguished by the precise and elegant patterns of the sculptural ornamentation which is evident also from a first superficial glance. The two central columns uphold the very beautiful finely-sculpted arch which is all that remains of the original triangular tympanum which once crowned the edifice. The ornamentation of the arch perpetuates the motifs of the friezes which are prominent on the entablature and culminate centrally in the *Bust of Tyche* (the Goddess who was protectress of the city). The architraved structure which stands out on the portals is embellished by a rich decoration drawing on classical motifs. Above the main portal which gives access to the naos is a semi-circular lunette which attracts the attention of the visitor because of its precious sculptured figurations: from an elegant interweaving of flowers and acanthus leaves, rises a female figure very similar to the classic effigies of *Medusa*. Inside the naos we can see a part of the original podium which once upheld the statue of Emperor Hadrian, venerated as a deity.

HOUSES ON THE SLOPE

From the opposite part of the Temple of Hadrian the interesting complex of the so-called "Houses on the slope" faces out onto the Street of the Curetes, inhabited by the most qualified and wealthy social class, and for this reason also known as «rich men's houses». Their particular position on the slopes of the mountain enabled each house to serve as a covered terrace for the one next to it.

The so-called **House of the Peristyle II** was in fact distinguished by the considerable profusion of decorations. Its dating is from the 1st century, even if it was rebuilt several times, at least until the 6th century. The numerous inside rooms have mosaic flooring and frescoes on the walls (4th century).

The **House of the Peristyle I** has been restored, like the previously-mentioned one, to give visitors a chance to realize what the general arrangement of these Ephesian

A frescoed wall in the House of the Peristyle II.

Facade and entrance staircase of the Library of Celsus.

Following page: a fascinating view from above of the Theatre, with the ruins of the Arcadian Way.

patrician residences had been. The building of this residence goes back to the 1st century as does the first mentioned one. The subjects of the paintings were inspired by theatrical motifs: it is for this reason that the room is known as "the theatre". Worthy of note are the motifs inspired by plays by Menander and Euripides, while other frescoes represent male and female nudes.

LIBRARY OF CELSIUS

The library was built during the Imperial Age, at the time of Hadrian, and was erected by Tiberius Julius Aquila who desired that it be dedicated to his father. The building was begun in 114, and was concluded in 135 by Tiberius J. Aquila's heirs, to whom a bequest of money was left so that they would provide for the purchase of books and for the maintenance of the complex.

In the second half of the 3rd century, at the time of the invasions by the Goths, the inside of the edifice was completely devastated by a fire which fortunately spared the external structures of the facade.

The facade is embellished with the scenic effect of two rows of columns. Those on the first floor, with Corinthian capitals, are arranged in four pairs at the summit

of the entrance staircase, made of nine steps. The columns of the upper floor are smaller than those on the lower floor. The columns of the three central pairs uphold architectural elements in the shape of triangular and semi-circular pediments. On the lower floor, behind the scenographic colonnade, three doors are framed by very fine ornamental motifs, in the manner of friezes in relief and surmounted by the same number of windows.

Following pages:

THE THEATRE

The theatre has come down to us in a wonderful state of preservation, and constitutes one of the best-preserved buildings in the entire archaeological zone. As with all similar constructions, the Ephesian theatre follows a division into three main sections: *skene* (the proscenium), *orchestra* (place for scenic action) and *cavea* (space reserved for the audience). The original theatre could seat about 24,000; the auditorium originally rose for at least 30 metres over the orchestra, and was crowned at the summit by a porticoed structure which had the function of further improving the acoustics in the complex.

The picturesque port of Kuşadasi.

KUŞADASI

The importance of this town, in a picturesque site overlooking the gulf of the same name stretching out towards the Aegean, depends as much on its atmosphere and landscape as it does on the fact that it is an ideal point of departure for excursions. Kuşadasi is in fact a charming seaside resort with good hotels and restaurants, as well as functional well-equipped international tourist complexes. The surroundings furnish the occasion to admire some of the most qualified and interesting archaeological sites in all of Turkey: from Ephesos to Priene, Miletus, Colophon. The spacious gulf of Kuşadasi is circumscribed on the north by an irregular peninsular appendix which separates it from the gulf of Izmir, terminating opposite the island of Chios. In the southern portion a promontory extends towards the island of Samos, leaving a narrow

arm of the sea open. In front of the inhabited center, on an isle connected by a road to the mainland, rises the **Kücükada Kalesi**, an ancient fortress still surrounded by imposing turreted glacis. This fortress became famous during the 16th century when it was used as base for the exploits of the pirate Khair ad-Din better known as *Barbarossa*. The famous corsair together with his brothers raged along the Aegean coasts of North Africa, and established a small kingdom in Algeria which served as a bridgehead for further conquests in the Mediterranean basin. After the occupation of Tunis (1533) the Turkish sultan Süleyman entrusted him with the command of the Ottoman fleet against Charles V and the marine republics of Venice and Genoa, which he long kept at bay, acquiring great prestige and riches.

A detail of the archaeological zone of Priene.

PRIENE

The archaeological zone of Priene is situated along the upper edge of the flood plain left by the waters of the Büyük Menderes (anc. Maeander).

The first historical mention refers to an ancient Ionian seat; apparently originally the city stretched out over a peninsula with two ports. At the beginning of the 6th century B.C. the philosopher Bias, considered one of the Seven Sages of antiquity, lived in Priene. Destroyed by the Persians at the beginning of the 5th century B.C., it was rebuilt around the middle of the 4th, thanks to the intervention of the Athenians whose fortunes it followed at length. A prosperous commercial port of call that developed around the Nauloco — its port —, it was subject to the rule of the sovereigns of Pergamon, before passing under Rome. In the late Roman period the importance of Priene waned, in part due to the progressive silting up of the sites with detritus brought in by the Büyük Menderes. During the Byzantine period the city was seat of an important diocese. The excavations are characterized by the strictly orthogonal ground plan projected by Hippodamus of Miletus (4th cent. B.C.). The **Agora** dates to the 3rd century B.C.; it comprised the center of city life and was surrounded by porticoes on three sides. Of great interest are the ruins of the **Temple of Athena**, surely one of the most beautiful examples of Ionian architecture in Asia Minor (4th cent. B.C.), unfortunately irreparably damaged by earthquakes and the weather. The **Theatre** was built in Hellenistic times (4th cent. B.C.) but was substantially restructured in Roman times (2nd cent. A.D.). Among the other significant vestiges of Priene mention should be made of the **Bouleuterion** and the **Prytaneion**, respectively the Senate and the seat of its executive committee; both can be dated around the middle of the 2nd century B.C.

The fine Ionian columns of the stoa in Miletus.

The majestic Theatre of Miletus still testifies to the past splendor of the city.

MILETUS

The ruins of the ancient city of Miletus lie on a hill encircled by the waters of the Büyük Menderes near the Aegean coast. As is the case with nearby Priene, the progressive accumulation of riverborn debris has played a considerable role in the city's historical and economical vicissitudes.

A large number of archaeological finds of the Mycenaean age indicate the existence of an old Mycenaean colony in the middle of the second millennium B.C. It became an important Ionian center of commerce and as its prosperity increased, Miletus established a large number of colonies throughout the Mediterranean area and along the coasts of the Black Sea. Culturally the city flourished and was the birthplace of the philosophers Anaximes and Anaximander, the historian and geographer Hecataeus, and the architects Hippodamos and Isidorus. When it fell into the hands of the Persians they razed it to the ground to punish its rebel tendencies. Some time later the city was rebuilt; as part of the Roman empire (2nd cent. B.C.) it once more acquired some of its ancient prestige, which however was rapidly threatened by the silting up of the port and the consequent loss in importance and decline of commercial activities. Archaeological investigation of the zone of Miletus, begun at the turn of the century, is still in course.

The most frequently visited attraction is the **Theatre**. Scenographically set against the hill, it was originally built around the 4th century B.C. and was enlarged in the Hellenistic period when it had a seating capacity of 5,300. Its present size is the result of a restructuration undertaken in Roman times (2nd cent. A.D.) which brought its seating capacity to a maximum of 15,000. Further on what is left of two lion structures set to guard the entrance to the port can still be seen. The remains of the **Sanctuary of the Delphic Apollo** represent the principal place of worship in the city. Built in the archaic period, the edifice was transformed in Doric style in the Hellenistic age; during Roman domination the porticoes were rebuilt in Corinthian style.

Other important vestiges include the **Bouleuterion** which was probably erected under Antiochus Epiphanes, king of Syria (second half 2nd cent. B.C.), the southern **Agora** (market place built in the Hellenistic age) and the **Stadium** (2nd cent. B.C.) which contained up to 15,000 spectators. Near the southern agora stands the **Ilyas Bey Camii**. This square mosque (15th cent.) has a dome and is notable for its fine architectural design as well as the profusion of fine marble inlays and for its decor. Particularly noteworthy is the prayer niche (*mihrab*).

The **Baths of Faustina** were named after the wife of Marcus Aurelius who donated them in the second half of the 2nd century A.D. The bath complex is extremely well preserved even though it does not fit into the urban network of orthogonal streets planned by Hippodamus. The central courtyard was surrounded by Corinthian columns. The *palaestra* could be reached through the dressing room (*apodyterium*) where the statues of the Muses, now in the **Museum** of Istanbul, were found. Of the rooms which were part of the bathing establishment itself mention can be made of the *frigidarium*, decorated with sculpture which served as a fountain for the pool in the center, the *calidarium* composed of two apsed rooms furnished with hypocausts for heating, and the *tepidarium*.

The evocative remains of what must have been a monument all of 18 meters high.

The imposing ruins of the Temple of Apollo in Didyma. Its oracle was famous throughout the Ancient world.

DIDYMA

In antiquity a *Sacred Way* connected Miletus to the port of Didyma and its famous temple. The last stretch of road was flanked by statues of sphinxes and reclining lions, now to be seen in the British Museum in London. This important street dating back at least to the 6th century B.C. confirms the hypothesis of the existence here of a small archaic temple, far earlier than the foundation of the colossal place of worship dedicated to Apollo. Traces of this original building have in fact been identified inside the large temple.

Evidence of the popularity of the sanctuary goes back to the archaic period, in particular from the 6th century B.C. on, when mention is made of gifts offered by the powerful and by kings, comparable to those offered to the famous oracle of Delphi. In line with what Pausanias affirms, it is highly likely that at Didyma, as in many other centers of Asia Minor, the Greeks replaced all forms of local cult with their own forms of worship. It seems to have been ascertained that the sacred place dedicated to Apollo existed before the first Ionic colonies settled here. Even the statue of *Apollo capturing a stag* found in the temple can be related to religious motifs of obvious Hittite and Anatolian extraction. Further evidence that a cult

of Apollo existed prior to Greek colonization is to be found in Homer's *Iliad*.

The history of archaeology regarding this temple is relatively recent, and dates back only to the 1960s. Excavations undertaken by German archaeologists led first to the identification of the foundations of a perimetral wall of the sanctuary, thought to have been built in the 8th or 7th century B.C. The subsequent discovery of a colonnade dating to the end of the 7th century B.C. leads to the supposition that the original nucleus was at the time enlarged. The first temple was burned by the Persians at the beginning of the 5th century B.C., but when Alexander the Great conquered the Anatolian regions, a much larger and more scenographic place of worship was built on the same site.

The **Temple of Apollo Didyma** is one of the largest of the Hellenistic classical period, preceded solely by the Artemision of Ephesus and the Temple of Hera in Samos. Still today an idea of the ancient splendor of the building with its impressive number of Ionic columns still transpires from these imposing magnificent ruins. Even though work on the temple complex continued from the 3rd century B.C. up to Roman times, it was never finished. The shrine itself was surrounded by a

Still more vestiges of the Temple of Apollo and an enormous relief with the head of Medusa.

portico with two rows of columns. Some of these architectural elements have withstood the ravages of time and the earthquakes and still stand in their solemn beauty, often complete with capitals and architraves. The shrine where prophecies were revealed in the name of Apollo was faced in marble brought from the Aegean islands. Of particular note among the numerous decorations found in the temple are various busts of divinities such as *Apollo, Jupiter, Artemis* and *Latona*, as well as capitals ornamented with heads of griffins and bulls, which, together with a *head of Medusa* that was part of a frieze on an architrave, are examples of 2nd century A.D. sculpture.

Not far from the temple, a **Stadium** surrounded by seven rows of seats has been identified. Apparently this installation was used for the sacred competitions which accompanied the religious rites held in the temple. Some of the tiers of seats are incised with names that belong to the late Hellenistic period.

The Castle of St. Peter in Bodrum, ancient Halicarnassus.

BODRUM

Bodrum, the ancient *Halicarnassus* or Halikarnassos in Greek, is today a pleasant vacation resort overlooking a charming bay admired by tourists and visitors for the purity and transparency of its limpid waters, for the amenities of its sandy beaches and the local microclimate that is particularly inviting and felicitious. The coastline of the picturesque gulf is varied by charming small peninsulas while the silhouettes of some of the Aegean islands stand out on the horizon.

According to Herodotus, the most famous son of Halicarnassus, the city was founded by Dorian colonists who later instituted the Dorian League. From the middle of the 6th century B.C. on, Halicarnassus was governed by the Persians, but it rebelled and adhered to the league of cities which had taken up arms against the oppressor. Around the middle of the 4th century B.C., with the advent of the reign of Mausolus, Halicarnassus and all of Caria experienced the period of their greatest splendor. When the sovereign died, his wife and sister rose to the throne, and decreed the construction of the imposing mausoleum which was counted as one of the Seven Wonders of the An-

cient World and of which only a few fragmentary traces survive. At the same time Artemisia gained possession of Rhodes, suffocating the ambitious pretensions for conquest of its inhabitants. In the second half of the 4th century B.C. Halicarnassus was ravaged by Alexander the Great and its inevitable decline began then, putting it at the mercy of the emerging powers. Archaeological excavations by various English specialists in the mid-19th century brought to light only fragments of reliefs and various statues. Nowadays practically nothing remains of the majestic monumental structure which aroused the admiration of Pliny, who has left us an accurate description. The **Mausoleum** (after Mausolus to whom it was dedicated) was built by Queen Artemisia around 350 B.C. The famous architect Pytheos, who had also designed the Temple of Athena in Priene, was called in to prepare the plans. The sculpture and fine reliefs in the friezes on the facade were commissioned from the most famous artists of the time, including Scopas, Bryaxis, Timotheus and Leocares. The monumental complex rose up on a high podium, with a row of Ionic columns

The typical port of Bodrum and an exhibition of carpets.

supporting a stepped pyramidal roof crowned by a marble quadriga. The majestic monument stood intact until the 12th century, but was partially destroyed by an earthquake in the 14th century. Its destruction continued in the same century when it was used as a quarry for the construction of the fortress which now rises from the waters of the bay. A few fragments of the frieze and the statues of *Artemisia* and *Mausolus*, once on the roof, driving the quadriga, are now to be seen in the British Museum in London.

In the **Marine Museum** of Bodrum, a recently discovered sculptured panel, once part of the frieze of the famous Mausoleum, is on view together with a number of objects found at the bottom of the sea, vases dating to the 9th-8th century B.C. and other Dorian material including a terracotta sarcophagus (9th cent. B.C.).

The so-called **Castle of St. Peter** stands in the center of the harbor and is one of the well-known features in the landscape of this pleasant town. The construction of its powerful glacis was begun by the Knights Hospitalers in the 15th century, using materials taken from the ruins of the Mausoleum. In 1523 the fortress once and for all fell into the hands of the Turks.

The lovely beach of Marmaris is right below densely wooded mountains.

MARMARIS

Despite the ancient origins and closeness of important archaeological sites (Knidos and Kaunos) which testify to the existence of a flourishing civilization on the coast in earliest times, Marmaris today is exclusively a tourist seaside resort. The town, which stands on the site of the ancient *Physkos* of which barely the memory remains, spreads out around a picturesque circular bay, with green mountains on all sides. The safe natural harbor, opposite which lie numerous enticing islands, has always furnished ships and boats with an ideal landing place. Today the yachts of an international clientele who favor this stretch of southern Turkey for vacations or as a base for interesting excursions into the environs are sheltered here. A seaside resort with a mild riviera climate, it is furnished with adequate receptive and tourist structures. A flourishing and dense Mediterranean flora offers a natural frame for the lovely farflung beaches. The only remembrance of the city's past is a **Fortress** built in the Ottoman period. Its mighty crenellated ramparts, together with a tower, stand out at the center of the promontory that stretches out towards the sea; all around are clusters of modern houses.

In Knidos, as in other sites in Turkey, the archaeological ruins overhang the blue of the sea.

KNIDOS

The setting of the archaeological zone of Knidos is particularly lovely, lying as it does at the lip of the promontory that stretches out to the west of Marmaris and theoretically separates the waters of the Mediterranean from those of the Aegean. According to a description made by Strabo, Knidos was built on a terraced slope, rather like an amphitheatre, from the coastline up to the highest point of the acropolis. The city had two ports, one of which was military in nature and could be closed as well as offering anchorage to a score of triremes. Despite the silting up of the docks, which today form a real isthmus, it has been possible to uncover evidence of the narrow canal which originally connected the northern and southern ports.

Knidos held an important position among the cities of the west coast of Asia Minor; it belonged to the Dorian Hexapolis and developed an intense trade and prosperous activities connected with the exportation of its ex-

cellent wines. The city was a center for the arts and culture; the birthplace of the architect Sostratus, who designed the Pharos or lighthouse of Alexandria, considered one of the wonders of the Ancient World, as well as of the astronomer and mathematician Eudoxus (5th cent. B.C.). The inhabitants of the city erected their treasury in Delphi in the second half of the 6th century B.C., while the wall frescoes in the Pecile of Knidos in Athens were admired for the fine painting by Polygnotos (mid-5th cent. B.C.).

The Hellenistic city walls of the ancient city have been preserved while the town plan reveals the project of Hippodamos of Miletus. Archaeological research in the second half of the 19th century has brought to light a fine statue of a *seated Demeter*, now in the British Museum, while various Roman copies give us an idea of what the stupendous *Aphrodite* by Praxitiles in the temple of Aphrodite must have looked like.

One of the petrified cascades of Pamukkale.

PAMUKKALE

North of Denizli a road leads to Pamukkale, the site of a unique natural phenomenon, and to the important archaeological zone of Hierapolis. The name Pamukkale means *Castle of Cotton* and this is particularly apt in describing one of the most extraordinary landscapes to be found in nature. Here, in a landscape fascinating in its own right, the action of various mineral springs which contain calcium oxides has left fantastic concretions on the travertine structures. The resulting effect is spectacular: these mineral-rich waters have dripped down over a series of terraced levels designing bizarre solidified cascades, dazzling in their radiance and changing their color according to how the sunlight strikes them. From a distance this whitish mass stands in evident contrast with the color of the surrounding uplands and brings to mind enormous stretches of cotton. On approaching this incredible succession of terraces, one discovers the existence of basins full of mineral water which flow into other natural basins below, and are the source of stupendous mineral conglomerations in the form of fantastic stalactites, sometimes of considerable size and resembling organ pipes. The continuous dynamics of erosion and transformation of the natural landscape has resulted in an ambience unequalled elsewhere and which constitutes one of the most unique phenomena to be found in nature. Hordes of wonderstruck tourists swarm daily through this fabulous lunar landscape. The excellent curative properties of the waters, known from ancient times in the neighboring Hierapolis, have permitted the construction in modern times of spas, generally annexed to the hotels in the area. The entire territory of Pamukkale is at the center of particular attention on the part of the competent authorities who intend to safeguard the integrity and respect of this truly unique territory.

Various aspects of the extraordinary landscape of the cascades of Pamukkale.

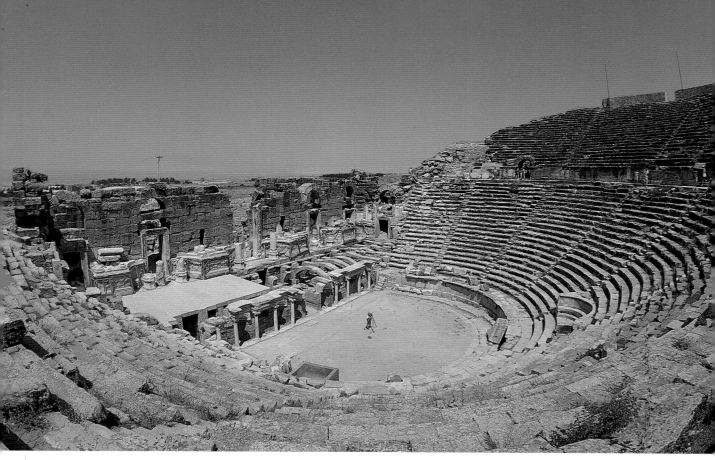

A view from above of the Theatre of Hierapolis.

HIERAPOLIS

The archaeological zone of Hierapolis stretches out in the surroundings of Pamukkale.

Traditionally the city was founded by the king of Pergamon Eumenes II. In the second half of the 2nd century B.C. Hierapolis passed to the Romans as provided for in the testament of Attalus III. The emperors took good care of the city, which was known for its baths and miracle-working hot springs. In 17 A.D. a terrible earthquake razed it to the ground but reconstruction soon began under Tiberius. The city flourished under the emperors who followed and the new Christian doctrine also found a fertile terrain thanks to the apostolate of Philip who was martyrized here in 80 A.D.

The **Roman Theatre** was built in the 2nd century A.D. and is still basically in good condition despite the collapse of much of the proscenium and the frons scenae. The cavea, which is set against the hillside, once had a seating capacity of 25,000 and is still used for representations in the Festival of Pamukkale.

The **Baths**, erected most probably in the 2nd century A.D., are in a good state of preservation and present the visitor with the sequence of what remains of the various rooms.

Not far off lies what is left of a two-apsed building with a single nave. It is generally believed to be a Christian **Basilica** built around the 6th century. The **Temple of Apollo** as we see it today dates back to the 3rd century and is the fruit of the reconstruction of a precedent Hellenistic temple, razed to the ground by an earthquake.

Other remains in this archaeological zone which merit attention include the so-called **Martyrium of St. Philip**, built in the early 5th century on an octagonal ground plan to house the mortal remains of the saint who was martyrized here during the persecutions ordered by Domitian. Outstanding in the list of attestations of Roman times in Hierapolis is the so-called **Arch of Domitian**, an imposing gateway with three passageways erected under Julius Frontinus who was proconsul in the Anatolian province in the 1st century A.D. Beyond the arch, before reaching the vast necropolis, the ruins of a bath structure dating to the 2nd-3rd century A.D. can be distinguished. It was later

The monumental gateway with three arches erected by the proconsol Julius Frontinus in the lst century A.D.

An example of an aedicule tomb with a pediment in the large necropolis of Hierapolis.

converted into a church (5th cent.). The **Necropolis** is one of the most extensive of its kind in all of Turkey. The burial grounds, which stretch out for almost two km. on either side of the way, contain an impressive number of tombs of various types and periods. Tumulus tombs, sarcophaguses and actual mausoleums date from the late Hellenistic to the Byzantine period.

APHRODISIAS

The important archaeological site of Aphrodisias is situated on a plateau at the foot of the mountain chain of Ak Dağ, not far from the valley through which the Büyük Menderes, the ancient *Meander*, runs. Nearby is the village of Geyre whose name has been interpreted by some as deriving from the name of the ancient region, *Caria*.

Archaeological research has confirmed the fact that the territory where one of the most important civilizations in Asia Minor was to develop was already inhabited in remote antiquity (Bronze Age). Among the many names given to the city, that of *Ninova* is obviously related to the Babylonian world. First mention of it as *Aphrodisias* dates only to the Hellenistic period. The city housed an important school of sculptors who settled in Pergamon, creating an extremely expressive and dynamic type of sculpture which was favorably received both in the Greek and Roman worlds. In the meanwhile the cult of Aphrodite had taken deep hold in Aphrodisias with characteristics similar to those of the Ephesos Artemis or Cybele, to cite other forms under which she was venerated when

the Hellenistic period was at its zenith, all with a common religious matrix. During Roman domination the city achieved the highest level of its splendor. Silla is known to have sent gifts in compliance with the answer of the oracle and was rewarded with privileges by Marc Antony and, later, by Tiberius. An intense flowering in the field of the arts and culture in general went hand in hand with the fame acquired by the religious cults. The spread of Christianity met with firm resistence in the city, tenaciously anchored to the ancient pagan cults. In the Byzantine period Aphrodisias, which in the meantime had become Stauropolis (*the City of the Cross*), acquired important administrative functions in the field of religion. Its decline and progressive abandonment was hastened in the 11th-13th centuries by the repeated Seljuk raids.

The archaeological discovery of Aphrodisias was begun early in the century by the French archaeologist Goudin. The most successful campaigns however where those undertaken in the early 1960s by Prof. K. T. Erim for New York University.

Near the entrance to the archaeological excavations,

enclosed in a late Roman (3rd cent. A.D.) circuit of **walls**, later consolidated, is the **Museum of Aphrodisias**. Numerous objects found during the excavations have been installed here: busts of emperors, reliefs formerly part of the *monument to Zoilos*, sculpture from the Roman and Byzantine periods, finds from prehistory and later, as well as a statue of a seated *Aphrodite*, some fine tombs and other examples of sculpture from the so-called school of Aphrodisias.

The beautiful **Theatre**, still in a good state of preservation and still used for representations, was brought to light near the **acropolis** where traces of prehistoric settlements have been found. Built in the lst century B.C. and used as an arena in the 2nd century A.D., the theatre could seat up to 10,000 spectators.

In the neighborhood of the *Portico of Tiberius* (1st century A.D.), destined for commerce, is the majestic complex of the **Baths of Hadrian** (2nd cent. A.D.) from which interesting architectural fragments and fine sculpture have come. Among the various rooms, the *palaestra* and those used for curative baths can be identified.

The **Agora** was dedicated to Tiberius (2nd cent. A.D.) and consisted of a large porticoed enclosure with Ionic columns. Interesting mosaics and statues were found in the **Odeion** (2nd-4th cent. A.D.) which must originally hve been larger than it is now.

The **Temple of Aphrodite** was built in the 1st century B.C. and enclosed in a *temenos* (sacred enclosure) in Hadrian's time (2nd cent. A.D.) . Its transformation into a basilica (6th cent.) by the Byzantines is still visible among the many surviving columns.

At the northern limits of the archaeological zone stands the imposing **Stadium** (1st-2nd cent. A.D.) with a seating capacity of 30,000 and later transformed into an arena. This is an outstanding example of a good state of preservation among buildings of this kind in the Anatolian area.

Fluted Ionic columns tell us of the great Temple erected in honor of Aphrodite.

The ancient Stadium of Aphrodisias could seat almost thirty thousand spectators.

The rock-cut tombs of Kaunos.

Panorama of the rock-cut tombs of Fethiye, the ancient Telmessos.

KAUNOS

According to Herodotos, the inhabitants of Kaunos considered themselves descendants of the Cretans even though they had evident origins in Caria. The presence of a port in the area is attested to as early as the 6th century B.C. Two centuries later the city was furnished with fortifications, and became an important center for trade and commerce which, thanks to its port, increased during the Hellenistic and Roman periods.

Architectural and structural elements of the so-called **Roman Theatre** are of evident Greek origin. The semicircular *cavea* is set against the side of the hill and the ruins of adjoining entrance buildings are still extant. In the vicinity of the port are the remains of a **Corinthian Temple** of Roman date, a **Nymphaeum** of the same period and a **Stoa** built in Hellenistic times.

Further up stand what is left of the **Roman Baths**, of a **Palaestra** almost certainly of the same period, a Byzantine place of worship, and various small Roman temples. Ancient rock-cut tombs have turned up in the surroundings. They may date to around the 4th century B.C. but were undoubtedly reused by the Romans.

FETHIYE

The exact origins of the ancient town of Telmessos, over which the modern town of Fethiye is built, are not known. Yet it was the largest town in Lycia and an influential member, during the 5th century B.C., of the Delian Confederacy.

Two earthquakes in 1956 and 1957 destroyed a large number of its ancient monuments. Fortunately the collection of **rock tombs** cut into the cliff has remained intact. In fact, it can be said that Fethiye boasts some of the best Lycian tombs in the region, going back to between the 6th and 3rd centuries B.C. In the place known as "Bademli Bahçe", meaning "garden of the almonds", one can admire the most spectacular tomb of the entire collection. "Tomb of Aminta" is engraved into the stone; it is dated the 4th century B.C. and imitates the shape and style of the Greek temple known as "templum in antis": in fact, the facade is formed by two Ionic capitals inserted between two pillars, supporting the decorated pediment. Behind is a false door divided into four panels.

The Aminta tomb and another Lycian tomb in Fethiye.

The Theatre of Pinara.

PINARA

The Lycian name of this ancient town was Pinale, meaning round. In fact, according to Manecrates — a 4th century historian —, the townsfolk of Xanthus thought that their city was overpopulated. So they split up into three groups, one of which settled on a height, founding Pinara. In any case, this town already existed during the 5th century B.C. Strabo maintained that the town was so important that it posed a threat to the Lycian Federacy together with Olympos, Myra, Tlos, Xanthus and Patara. It was conquered, together with the latter two by Alexander the Great in 334 B.C. Pinara is full of all types of tombs some of which feature pillars with facades hewn out of the rock. The **theatre** is also in a good state of repairs. Dating back to the 2nd century B.C., it could accommodate 3,200 spectators and consists of 27 rows divided into nine wedgeshaped sectors by ten flights of steps.

LETOON

Recently the remains of Letoon came to light a few kilometers from Xanthus; seat of the most famous sanctuary of Lycia, as its name suggests, it was dedicated to the goddess Latona — loved by Jove — and to her famous sons Apollo and Artemis.

On can still see the ruins of the **three temples**, most probably dedicated to these three gods: the most ancient one, which goes back to the 4th century B.C., is built between the other two in Ionic and Doric style. Apart from the Greek theatre, they also brought to light a huge nymphaeum formed by two buildings separated by a pool.

The remains of imposing pluted columns lie on the ground where the temples dedicated to Latona, Apollo and Artemis once stood.

The northern portico of the Nymphaeum in Letoon.

The Theatre of Xanthus with, on the left, the Tomb of the Harpies.

Two pictures of the lovely coast near Patara, modern Kelemiş.

XANTHUS

The name Xanthus brings Homer to mind: in fact the river, which bears the same name and which in Greek means yellow, is mentioned in the Iliad because it is from here that Arpedonte left at the head of his troups. Today the valley is known as Esen Cay. Discovered in 1838 by the archaeologist Charles Fellows, it is the oldest town in Lycia and must have existed at the time of the epic war described by Homer.

Its name is also associated with another event: it was a free, independent town until 545 B.C., when it was besieged by the Persian army led by Harpagus. When they saw they were doomed to defeat they preferred to take their lives rather than fall to the enemy. According to Herodotus, the men first of all killed the women and children, before setting fire to the citadel where they had gathered together all their worldy possessions. They then swore to fight to the death, and did. Besieged in 42 B.C. by Brutus, it was sacked and its citadel destroyed; only 150 inhabitants survived. Later on, it reacquired considerable importance from the trading and political points of view, but the Arab depredations were the coup de grâce.

Alongside the **theatre**, which dates back to the 2nd century A.D. but was probably built over a previous Greek theatre, stands the famous **Tomb of the Harpies**, whose original reliefs are kept in the British Museum in London.

PATARA

Patara is famous on two accounts: as the birth-place of St. Nicholas who has entered into Christian tradition as Father Christmas and for having long been the seat of a famous oracle to Apollo.

It was Herodotus who wrote about the importance of the oracle, second only to that of Delphi: it only functioned, so to speak, during the six winter months, when the God sojourned there; Apollo spent the remaining six summer months at the Delphic Oracle.

Founded, according to legend, by Patarus, son of Apollo and the nymph Lycia during the 5th century B.C., its Lycian name was Pttara or Pttaraze. It was also called Arsinae, when it fell under Egyptian rule and Ptolemy II changed its name in honour of his sister whom he also married.

Thanks to its geographic position, it was one of the main trading and naval ports of Lycia, before it was entirely silted up to form a wide beach.

Access is gained to the town through a three-gated **monumental arch**, erected in 100 A.D. and whose corbels bore busts of the members of the family of Mettius Modestus, Roman governor of Lycia. The **theatre**, partly dug out of the sand hill, goes back to the 2nd century A.D. and, as we can read in an inscription on the stage wall, it was extended and embellished by Velia Procula in 147 A.D.

Kaş is one of the most famous tourist resorts along the south coast of Turkey.

KAŞ

Coming from inland, we are dazzled by the magnificent view from above the bay of Kaş, one of the most famous tourist resorts along the southern coast of Turkey. But it is also famous from the historic point of view because Kaş was originally the ancient town of *Antiphellus*, harbour of the town of Phellus which stood in front of it.

Founded during the 6th century B.C., it soon became an important trading port and — according to Pliny — it was used for exporting wood from the green forest that covered Lycia. On the top of the hill, offering a view over the creeks and inlets, stands the Greek **theatre**, built during the 1st century B.C. but probably extended during the 3rd century A.D. It is very small and has 26 rows of seats divided into three sectors, with the cavea much larger than the usual semicircle. Its proportions, excellent condition and panoramic position have made it one of the most outstanding monuments along this stretch of the coast.

KEKOVA

The long, narrow island of Kekova and archaeological sites that surround it are one of the most characteristic settings along this part of the coast.

Separated from the mainland by an arm of sea, since ancient times it has been safe for anchoring: once upon a time for pirate or Roman ships, and nowadays for the tourist boats that find a dream-world here.

The ancient towns of Aperloi, Simena and Teimiussa have been turned into ruins, partly submerged by the water; therefore one can swim in the crystal clear water brushing against remains of walls or a Lycian sarcophagus which seems to emerge from the waves as if by magic. Very few other places have managed to blend in so well the charm and fascination of antiquity with the pleasure of life that passes serenely and timelessly in these little fishing villages.

The village of Simena: a Lycian sarcophagus rises almost miraculously from the clear waters of the sea.

Archaeological ruins in the village of Tersane.

On Kekova island the ruins run right down into the sea.

The exterior of the church of St. Nicholas.

DEMRE

The present-day town of Demre — Myra in antiquity — boasts a very touching historic and architectural feature: the **Church of St. Nicholas**.

Born in Patara in about 300 A.D., St. Nicholas studied in Xanthus and became bishop in Myra, where he preached until he was martyred in 325 A.D., during the Diocletian persecutions. He was buried in this church built along Byzantine lines: three apses preceded by an atrium and a double narthex, with frescoes and mosaic flooring. Immediately after his death, visitors to his tomb were miraculously cured; that is how Myra became a sacred place and destination of pilgrims. Destroyed and rebuilt several times, the church was sacked by vandals following on the Arab incursion in 1034. It was then surrounded by a protective wall by order of the Emperor Constantine Monomacus IX and his wife Zoë. Lastly, in 1087, Italian traders took the saint's bones to Bari, where he was proclaimed patron of the town. Legend has it that when the Italian traders opened the sarcophagus containing the saint's remains, they were overwhelmed by a strong scent of myrrh, which emanated from his bones. By virtue of another legend, St. Nicholas became the patron saint of children to whom he brings Christmas presents.

This is a place of great interest for Christianity if it is also true that St. Paul met here with the apostles for the last time before going to Rome.

The superb necropolis of Myra, with the tombs hewn out of the rock.

MYRA

A couple of kilometers north of Demre, the ruins include a score of tombs arranged on the cliff in a jumble overlooking the sea; perhaps this is the most amazing collection of rock tombs in the whole of Anatolia. Myra comes from the Greek word "mirra"; we know for certain that it dates back at least as far as the 5th century B.C. and was one of the most important towns in the Lycian Federation. Its superiority lasted in time; in fact, during the Byzantine era Theodosius II promoted it to capital of Lycia. Unfortunately, its promotion coincided with the Arab predations that commenced during the 7th century and continued for over two centuries. In 809, Myra was conquered by Harun el-Rashid and the city was gradually abandoned.

Evidence of its glorious past are the rock tombs dating back to the Lycian era and the Greco-Roman theatre. On the subject of its unique **necropolis**, it was a Lycian custom to bury their dead high up because they believed that in this way they were more easily transported to heaven. These funeral monuments date from the 6th to the 3rd century B.C.: built isolatedly or cut out of the rock-face, several of the facades have flat or sloping roofs carved to imitate wooden beams supported by pillars, suggesting that they are copied in form from wooden temples; the Greek temple is revealed by the rich decorated architraves. The richness of decorations — some still have traces of color — and in particular the magnificence of sculptured bas-reliefs, usually portraying the dead person surrounded by his family, testify to the exceptional taste and artistic sense of local artists for the time.

The same decorative taste can be found in the **theatre**, built in Greek style, that is, against a hill with fourteen flights of steps dividing the cavea in thirteen sectors, with twenty-nine rows of seats in the lower part and nine in the upper.

Here too the stage wall featured bas-reliefs with garlands, friezes and theatrical masks.

View of the Theatre of Arykanda, set against the hillside.

The arches of the aqueduct in the midst of a cluster of green pines.

Detail of the cavea of the ancient Theatre of Phaselis.

ARYKANDA

We know very little about the origins of this town, whose ending in "anda" leads us to believe that it was originally Anatolian. Before the 4th century B.C., its history is uncertain. It then came under a series of foreign conquests and dominations: firstly the Persians, then Alexander the Great, followed upon his death by the Seljuks; lastly after 43 A.D., it followed the fate of the rest of Lycia and joined the Roman Empire. Arykanda — which in Byzantine times was called Akalanda — was built on terraces on the slopes of Mount Akdag: the place is highly evocative, with its ruins that rise above the greenery and dominate the valley below.

The highest of these terraces was occupied by the **stadium** of the Hellenistic age: from here steps led down to the **theatre**, built against the hill during the 2nd century A.D. and in excellent condition; it has twenty rows of seats, divided into seven sections.
The lowest terrace features the complex of **baths**, which is still virtually intact in its sequence of arches. Water was supplied to Arykanda by means of a complex of four canals hewn out of the living rock at various levels. The city also had two **necropolises**: one of these is particularly interesting because it still has a series of funeral monuments that are almost intact and countless richly decorated sarcophagi.

PHASELIS

The old village of Phaselis, now Tekirova, has always been associated with the sea. Founded by Rhodes at the beginning of the 6th century B.C., it soon became an important harbor, as can be deduced from the ships portrayed on coins. Strabo mentions three harbors: one in the north, one in the north-east and one in the south. One can still recognise the remains of the wall which protected the city's leading harbor like a dyke. However, the ruins of the most important buildings of Phaselis, barely covered today by the lush vegetation, lie between the later two ports.

The **theatre** dates back to the 2nd century A.D., but it is highly likely that it was preceded by an analogous building. Small and elegantly proportioned, with a cavea gently sloping down the side of the hill, it can seat 1,500 spectators.

The arches of the **aqueduct** that supplied the city stand out among the green of the pines. The water supply to Phaselis was assured also by a series of rainwater tanks.

Lastly, one can admire the **baths** and the paved road that leads to a **gate** erected in honor of the emperor Hadrian. But before leaving, a glance must be directed towards the massive and powerful Tahtali, 2,575 meters high, which dominates the surrounding landscape.

The tourist port in Kemer is one of the best equipped along the entire coast.

KEMER

With Kemer, ancient city and now a growing resort town with tourist villages hidden in the woods surrounding the bay, one takes a step back into mythology. Homer narrates in the VI book of the Iliad that it was the dwelling-place of Chimaera, the fire-breathing monster, part lion, goat and serpent, which gave it its name. The hero Bellerophon, astride Pegasus, defeated it by sticking his lead-lined sword into its throat, but its flames were not extinguished and still burn on the small mountain, known as Yanartas meaning volcano: it is, as a matter of fact, only a jet of natural gas which catches fire when it comes into contact with the open air, creating a fantastic effect especially at night. However, the mythological explanation is much more appealing and convincing!

Near Kemer are the remains of ancient **Olympos**, founded during the 3rd century B.C. and pirates' den before becoming part of the Roman Empire.

Surrounded by a luxuriant park, the town is named after the high mountain ten kilometers away which reaches a height of 2,400 meters.

One can still admire the remains of the baths, agora and basilica, apart from countless funeral monuments and interesting sarcophagi in Olympos.

The crystal-clear waters around so-called ''mouse island''.

The small tourist port of Antalya.

The "fluted minaret" is perhaps the town's most characteristic monument.

ANTALYA

The snow-capped peaks of the Taurus mountain chain crown this charming bay, where the turquoise sea reflects the lush vegetation consisting of palm-trees, oleanders and lemon-trees.

Antalya, or Adalia as it is called nowadays, is the center of the coastal strip famous for its tourism; with its modern hotel facilities, sports grounds, tourist harbor and numerous camping grounds, Antalya boasts evergrowing numbers of tourists, who are attracted by its historic and artistic heritage and civilization, together with its spectacular scenery. Antalya is one of the few cities existing today whose ground was inhabited in remote times. Teeth, arrow-heads, and various utensils have been discovered which date back as far as 50,000 years. The entire region has been occupied by

indigenous peoples since 1200 B.C. until it was colonized by the Greeks who intermarried with the locals.

Antalya was founded in 159 B.C. by King Attalus of Pergamon who gave it its name: Attaleia. However, the Crusaders called it Satalia. The city only took on its present name under the dominion of the sultan Alâeddin Keykubat, who made it his winter residence. In 130 A.D., the emperor Hadrian, a great traveller, honoured the city with a visit; to commemorate the occasion, they built the city's most outstanding monument: **Hadrian's gate**. Most imposing in its grandeur, the gate opens with three supporting arches and columns crowned by Corinthian capitals. It must have originally been built in two stories and have been sur-

Two views of Hadrian's Gate, built in honor of the Roman emperor who visited Antalya in 130 A.D.

rounded by statues of the emperor and his family. The arch provides access to the town: or should we say the "towns" because Antalya consists of the old town with its old wooden madrases (typical Seleucidan structures) and picturesque corners where time stands still and the pulsating, more modern town with its palmshaded boulevards, exotic gardens overhanging the sea and charming little ports where a fishing-boat is moored alongside a tourist yacht. Overlooking these two towns, we shall notice that they are dominated by an unusual minaret, whose turquoise majolica exterior has disappeared showing its brick lining. **Yivli Minare**, or grooved minaret, 37 meters high, was built at the beginning of the 13th century. The original mosque no

longer exists. You will notice another strange sight: the "broken minaret" of **Kesik Minare Cami**. In fact, the tapered minaret of the mosque was struck by lightning. The latter was originally a Byzantine basilica with three naves dedicated to Our Lady. The finds from all over Antalya are exhibited in the **Archaeological Museum**. Sarcophagi and statues, votive figures and architectural friezes, ceramics and mosaics are lined up in the garden and halls. It is worth mentioning a mosaic from Xanthus depicting the goddess Tethys holding her son Achilles by the heel; she is dipping him into the Styx river to ensure his invulnerability. How can one not recall Homer and the Iliad and the names of all Greek heroes in this land of conquest?

*Garlands, putti and festoons to be seen in the lovely
Museum in Antalya which was inaugurated
in April of 1985.*

Two pictures of the tourist port of the city.

An avenue in Antalya's large park.

The beach of Konyaalti with its polished pebbles stretches westwards for kilometers: in the background the snow-capped peaks of the mountain of Bey.

The spectacular waterfall formed by the Düden River lies about 14 kilometers northeast of Antalya.

The Theater of Termessos, built at an altitude of 1050 m.

TERMESSOS

Termessos is located on a natural plateau flanked by two mountains at 1050 meters above sea level; it is one of the best preserved archaeological sites in Turkey and the only town that Alexander the Great never managed to conquer. Certain inscriptions lead us to believe that its townsmen were emigrants from Lycia, who thought this was an ideal place to build a town. Walled only on two sides, Termessos' best defence lies in the mountain and the steep valley below. Its natural impregnability is enhanced by its exceptional water supply, which is quite unique if you think of the place and conditions under which it was built: a series of five tanks (7 m deep and at the most 11 m wide) were fed by a duct cut into the rock. In 334 B.C., Alexander decided that it was too risky to tackle the town and passed on.

During the 2nd and 3rd centuries B.C., Termessos was at the peak of its glory and boasted as many as 150,000 inhabitants: most of its buildings also date back to this period. Later on, it was severely damaged by an earthquake and gradually became less populated until it was completely deserted in the 7th century A.D.

Of all the ruins, the most impressive by far is the **theatre**; hewn out of the rock, it offers a view as far as Antalya. Built during the Hellenistic era, with its *frons scenae* opened by five doors, it featured twenty-seven rows of steps and could seat up to 4,000 spectators.

An outstanding feature of Termessos remains the large number of **tombs**, all around the slopes to the east, west and south. Some are hewn out of the rocks while others are in the form of sarcophagi mounted on high pedestals. The latter, scattered among the bushes in the valley, date back to the 2nd and 3rd centuries B.C.

PERGE

Joined to the sea in ancient times by the Kestros River — navigable at the time — Perge is one of the most important and spectacular coastal towns; it is also famous from the religious point of view because it was here that St. Paul delivered his first sermon, and from the historic standpoint because it is the birth-place of the mathematician Apollonius, author of a famous treatise on geometry.

The name Perge comes from an Anatolian dialect; nonetheless, in ancient times the townsmen believed that it had been founded by Greek heroes after the siege of Troy.

The first settlement dates back to 1000 B.C. and was probably located on the acropolis. Subsequently, it extended to the underlying plain.

Perge was a free and independent town until the arrival of Alexander the Great in 334 B.C.; it was already walled at the time. It prospered during the Hellenistic and Roman eras; during the 2nd century B.C., it minted coins featuring the statue of the Artemis of Perge, the major cult of the city. Having flourished during the first three centuries of imperial Rome, it went into a decline during the Byzantine era. Access is gained to the lower part of the town through **three gates**, of which the southern one, which dates back to the Hellenistic era, is the most majestic. Flanked by two round towers, its oval courtyard inside was transformed into a sort of court of honor in 120 A.D.; its walls were covered with precious marble slabs and its niches housed statues of the gods, the em-

The main street of ancient Perge, divided in two by a drainage canal.

Three views of the large city Gate, with its characteristic oval shape: in Turkish it is known as Oval Avlulu Kapi.

peror's family, the mythical founders of Perge and celebrities of the Roman world. This remarkable renovation was made possible through the generosity of Plancia the Great, the only woman in Perge who held an important office. From here one could head in the direction of the Acropolis. Perge was cut into quadrants by two colonnaded streets which intersected at right angles and which both date back to the 2nd century A.D. Halfway down each street, which was 20 meters wide, there was a water channel.

The Theater of Perge, built in 100 B.C. and with an audience capacity of 12,000.

The interior of the famous Theater of Aspendos, with the covered gallery at the top of the tiers of seats.

ASPENDOS

The present-day Belkiz was once situated on the banks of the River Eurymedon, now known as the Köprü Çay. In ancient times it was navigable; in fact, according to Strabo, the Persians anchored their ships there in 468 B.C., before the epic battle against the Delian Confederation.

It is commonly believed that Aspendos was founded by colonists from Argos. One thing is certain: right from the beginning of the 5th century, Aspendos and Side were the only two towns to mint coins. An important river trading port, it was occupied by Alexander the Great in 333 B.C. because it refused to pay tribute to the Macedonian king. It became an ally of Rome af-

ter the Battle of Sipylum in 190 B.C. and entered the Roman Empire.

The town is built against two hills: on the "great hill" or Büyük Tepe stood the acropolis, with the agora, basilica, nymphaeum and bouleuterion or "council chamber". Of all these buildings, which were the very hub of the town, only ruins remain. About one kilometer north of the town, one can still see the remains of the Roman **aqueduct** that supplied Aspendos with water, transporting it from a distance of over twenty kilometers, and which still maintains its original height.

Aspendos' **theatre** is the best preserved Roman theatre

A panorama of the Theater of Aspendos, with the imposing front of the stage.

anywhere in Turkey. It was designed during the 2nd century A.D. by the architect Zeno, son of Theodore and originally from Aspendos. Its two benefactors — the brothers Curtius Crispinus and Curtius Auspicatus — dedicated it to the Imperial family as can be seen from certain engravings on the stones. Discovered in 1871 by Count Landskonski during one of his trips to the region, the theatre is in excellent condition thanks to the top quality of the calcareous stone and to the fact that the Seljuks turned it into a palace, reinforcing the entire north wing with bricks. Its thirty-nine tiers of steps — 96 meters long — could seat about twenty thousand spectators. At the top, the elegant gallery and covered arcade sheltered spectators. One is immediately struck by the integrity and architectural distinction of the stage building, consisting of a *frons scaenae* which opens with five doors onto the proscenium and scanned by two orders of windows which also project onto the outside wall. There is an amusing anecdote about the construction of this theatre — in which numerous plays are still held, given its formidable acoustics — and the aqueduct just outside the town: in ancient times, the King of Aspendos had a daughter of rare beauty named Semiramis, contended by two architects; the king decided to marry her off to the one who built an important public work in the shortest space of time. The two suitors thus got down to work and completed two public works at the same time: the theatre and the acqueduct. As the sovereign liked both buildings, he thought it right and just to divide his daughter in half. Whereas the designer of the acqueduct accepted the Solomonic division, the other preferred to grant the princess wholly to her rival. In this way, the sovereign understood that the designer of the theatre had not only built a magnificent theatre — which was the pride of the town — , but would also be an excellent husband to his daughter; consequently he granted him her hand in marriage.

SIDE

According to Strabo, during the second half of the 7th century B.C., Greek colonists from an Ionian city settled there.

The Greek settlers immediately gave considerable impetus to the city's development. Side was an excellent port and trade flourished. Not only did the city prosper with piracy — widely diffused at the time — but also with its slave trade; its female slaves were renowned for their beauty even in Syria.

Due to the fact that Sideans never fell foul of Rome, Side was left in peace during the 2nd and 1st centuries B.C. It reached its moment of glory later on, during the 1st century and first half of the 2nd century A.D.: during this era it was embellished and enriched with outstanding monuments. The depredation of the Arabs during the 9th century put an end to Side, and it gradually dwindled in importance before being completely abandoned.

Despite several earthquakes, Side has preserved the majority of its buildings. One of the most important is the one erected in honor of the Emperor Vespasian and his son Titus. When it was restored, it was transformed into a fountain.

Side's importance in antiquity can also be deduced from the fact that the city possessed two **Agoras**.

Side's largest building was the **theatre**. It was built during the mid-2nd century A.D. with a technique which was quite exceptional for those times. The peculiarity of this monument lies in the fact that, unlike other theatres in the region, it is not Greek (built against a hill) but Roman: that is, built on flat land, it required vaulted constructions to support the tiers. The majority of statues found here are now housed in the city **Museum**, which was set up in 1964 in the Roman Baths, dating back to the 5th century A.D.

The monumental gate and the fountain dedicated to the emperor Vespasian in Side.

The Archaeological Museum of Side: architrave frieze with heads of Medusa, and the lid of a sarcophagus with the figures of the deceased couple on top.

The fortified walls of Alanya.

ALANYA

From above, Alanya is the most spectacular setting along the southern Anatoliam coast. What is nowadays the best equipped, busiest tourist harbor in Turkey was in ancient times a famous naval base, known as Korakesion. Founded in the 4th century B.C., under the Roman Empire it became a famous pirates' den.

During the 13th century, it was annexed to the kingdom of the great Seljuk sovereign, Alâeddin Keykubat who, having driven away the Byzantines, married the daughter of the defeated governor and made Korakesion his winter residence. The sultan also changed its name, to Alâya and then to its present name, Alanya. The **arsenal** dates back to this period; it is the only one of its kind from the Seljuk period that is still standing, with its elegant brick arches, marble entrance, servants' quarters and mosque.

However, the most important architectural feature of the town is the complex of walls, eight kilometers long, of the Byzantine fortress which dominates the town. They took twelve years to build; of the fifty towers, the most imposing is the **Kizil Kule or Red Tower**. 29 meters high, it was built in 1225 in an octagonal shape along the lines of cruciform fortifications. It owes its

141

Kizil Kule, or the Red Tower, with the port in the background.

Two pictures of the fortified citadel of Alanya. It is said that this is where the Romans threw those condemned to death into the sea.

name to the ruddy color of the stone blocks in the lower part and the bricks in the upper part. It was to defend the harbor of Alanya and its nearby arsenal; the spouts from which they poured boiling oil or tar over the enemy jut out from its massive structure.

Pirate raids that characterized Alanya's history also left their mark in the numerous caves in the vicinity, many of which can be reached only by boat. In the Kizlar Magarasi, pirates are said to have hidden the women they abducted during their incursions.

The most famous of all is **Damlataş Cave**. It is small

in size yet steeped in history, dating back about 15,000 years.

Situated on the eastern side of the crag of Alanya, it seems an unreal world in which stalactites, stalagmites and calcareous concretions combine to form a forest of petrified shapes.

With a constant temperature of 22 to 23 °C and a humidity content of 90 to 98 per cent, Damlataş Cave has the properties to heal asthma and other respiratory disorders.

The Alanya Arsenal, set against the hill, and another view of the sea.

The remains of ancient Seleucia, modern Silifke.

SILIFKE

Silifke is a prevalently modern town that grew up near the vestiges of the ancient *Seleucia al Calicadno*.

The city was founded on the lower banks of the Calicadno in the 3rd century B.C. by Seleucus I. In the second half of the 1st century A.D. the Roman governor L. Octavius Memor raised a bridge in honor of the emperor Vespasian and his sons. On June 10, 1190, the Third Crusade was dramatically brought to a halt when Emperor Frederick I Barbarossa drowned.

The town is dominated by the ruins of an imposing medieval **Fortress** (12th cent.) standing on the site of the ancient acropolis. The panorama from the glacis is marvelous while inside the fort traces of a mosque are to be found. Slightly further down is a large **cistern** of Roman times cut out of the rock and long used to supply Seleucia with water.

Remains of ancient buildings, none of which date to before the Romans, include the fragmentary ruins of a **Theatre** and a vast necropolis. Much more notable are the vestiges of the **Temple of Jupiter** erected in the 2nd century A.D., where some of the Corinthian columns with their capitals are still standing.

Mention must also be made of the **Ulu Camii** or *Great Mosque*, built by the Seljuk Turks, and an **Archaeological Museum** containing Greek sculpture of the 4th-2nd centuries B.C., bronzes, glass, a collection of coins and documentation of ethnographical interest.

KIZKALESI

The coastal road that joins Mersin to Silifke is particularly fascinating in those spots where the haunting scenery and the reminiscences of the past fuse into one. This is the case with Korykos, where Cicero had his headquarters when he lived in Asia Minor as governor, and now a popular tourist and seaside resort. A base for the exploration of a highly interesting archaeological zone, its fame derives from the presence of two ancient fortresses.

The most striking is without doubt the **Kizkalesi** which rises up from an extraordinarily blue crystal-clear sea in an unforgettable landscape setting. This structure, known also as *Castle of the Sea or of the Maiden*, dates to the 12th century even though apparently shelters of some kind already existed here in ancient times and were used by pirates and strengthened by the Romans, the Byzantines and the Ottoman Turks who took control in the second half of the 15th century.

Cylindrical towers rise up over the mighty glacis and inside there is a vast court with a chapel. Its name, Castle of the Maiden, refers to a legend which tells of a young princess who was imprisoned within its walls to save her from an obscure prophecy that she would die from the bite of a poisonous snake. However, despite all cautionary measures, the prophesy came true, for an asp was hidden in a basket of fruit sent by one of her suitors.

The second fortress, known also as *Castle of the Land*, rises on the mainland and was built in the 12th century employing material from other structures. It was used by Venetian and Genoese merchants who found it an ideal site for their trading activities. A few frescoed churches can be seen inside the castle. Of old, a dam thrown across the waters of the sea put it into contact with Kizkalesi.

The castle of Kizkalesi, built on an island, is within easy reach for the swimmer.

Adana, the principal Turkish center for the cotton industry.

ADANA

The city is one of the most populous cities in Turkey and is situated in a strategically important location, overlooking a vast plain in the south-eastern part of the country. A commercial and industrial center and communications crossroads, the chief city of Cilicia controls an ample agricultural territory known as *Cukurova*. Once covered with swamps and bogs and therefore unhealthy and full of malaria, the region was drained by careful regulation of the hydrograpic basin of the Seyhan River. The reclaimed land now furnishes cotton, citrus fruits, tobacco, vegetables, bananas, linen and sesame seeds in grat quantity. Upstream from the city a large artificial lake was formed which is used in irrigating the fields.

Its earliest origins date to the Hittite period (14th cent. B.C.) but there is mention of a Greek settlement as early as the 10th century B.C. In the 7th century B.C. the city fell into the hands of the Assyrians, subsequently (2nd cent. B.C.) it became part of the kingdom of Antiochus IV Epiphanes and then passed to the Romans, the Byzantines, the Seljuk Turks and the Mamelukes (14th cent.). Taken by the Ottoman Turks in the 16th century, it remained in Turkish hands with the exception of a temporary period of annexation to Egypt (first half 19th cent.) and a brief period of French oc-

cupation at the end of World War I.

Despite the complex vicissitudes of its ancient history, the city has no particularly important vestiges of the past. Noteworthy is the **Roman Bridge** known locally as Tas Köprü, thrown across the Seyhan River by Hadrian in the 2nd century A.D. Restored in Justinian's time, a goodly number of its original arches are still standing.

The **Ulu Camii**, or *Great Mosque*, was commissioned in the 16th century by the Ramazanoglu family. The building, which also contains a *madrasa*, distinguishes itself for the lovely majolica decoration from Iznik and Kütahya. Other mosques in the city are the **Esky Yag Camii** (15th cent.) with its fine portal, and the **Akça Mesçidi**, also of the 15th century.

A large number of extremely interesting archaeological finds are on display in the **Archaeological Museum**. They range from prehistory to the Ottoman period, with in particular sarcophaguses of various periods, sculpture, funerary steles, mosaics from the Roman period, objects of Hittite provenance and ceramics of Ottoman make. Other museums in the city worthy of mention are the **Ethnographical Museum** and the **Atatürk Museum**.

The Taş Köprü was built at the beginning of the 2nd century A.D. The arches, 310 meters long and 13 high, span the Seyan River.

KARATAŞ

A typical fishing village, Karataş overlooks the Mediterranean from the edge of a densely cultivated vast plain, south of Adana. It is also a highly rated seaside resort which benefits greatly from the fact that it is not yet frequented by the hordes of tourists elsewhere associated with mass tourism. Its waters are extraordinarily clear, with fascinating transparencies and enticing reflections. There is a special charm to the surrounding territory characterized by the presence of vast extensions of water. Nature is in its element here and the fauna includes rare and interesting species such as aquatic tortoises and chamaeleons, which provide an extra attraction for nature lovers. Structures for reception are decidedly limited, but the exquisite local dishes of fresh seafood in which a freshly caught fish becomes a major gastronomical event are to be had at low cost.

ANTAKYA

A medium sized city in southeast Turkey, it stretches out, not far from the Syrian border, in a flourishing plain washed by the waters of the Asi Nehri River. In antiquity the river was known as the *Orontes*, and *Antioch*, which lay on its banks then as now, became one of the most important and illustrious cities in the Near East.

Foundation dates to the end of the 4th century B.C. and is attributed to Seleucus I Nicator, a general under Alexander the Great. It grew rapidly and became one of the most flourishing and powerful cities in Asia Minor. Its star shone so brightly that it became the third city in the vast empire controlled by Rome. A center for the diffusion of the Christian doctrine, the apostles Peter and Paul both preached here and it was then a bishop's seat, long sustaining the Arian heresy. Destroyed by a serious earthquake in the first half of the 6th century, it was rebuilt under Justinian. In 1098, at the time of the Crusades, it became a principality governed by the son of Robert Guiscard, Boemondo. The prosperous development of this new institution was interrupted by the devastation brought on by the Mamelukes (second half 13th cent.). Part of the Ottoman territories after 1516, it was annexed to the modern Turkish state in 1939, after a period of French administration at the end of World War I.

Of interest for the visitor are the **Ulu Camii** (16th cent.), the **Habib Neccar Camii**, once a church and subsequently transformed into a mosque, and the so-called **Grotto of St. Peter**, an ancient rock-cut place of worship used by the Christians, and the collections in the **Archaeological Museum**, with architectural elements and sculpture, and elegant Roman mosaics.

An elegant mosaic preserved in Antakya.

The remains of the fortified Urartian city of Cavuştepe.

The lovely church of Akdamar near Lake Van, erected in 915.

The Castle of Mahmudiye, in Hosap, is a Kurd fortress built in 1643.

VAN

The site of the modern city of Van was already inhabited by man at the dawn of civilization.

The foundation of the ancient *Thospitis* dates to the 9th century B.C. Before long it became the capital of the kingdom of Urartu, was destroyed in the 7th century B.C., after which foreign occupation, begun under the Medes, continued unbrokenly until the arrival of the Arabs. Taken by the Seljuk Turks (11th cent.) and once more laid waste by the hordes of Tamerlane (14th cent.), it finally fell to the Ottoman Turks who defended it from claims on the part of the Persians.

A medieval **Fortress** looks down on the city, there where the acropolis of Thospitis once stood. The vestiges of ancient Urartian fortifications were encountered of archaeological excavations.

In the new city there is an interesting **Achaeological Museum**. A visit is absolutely essential to anyone interested in the ancient kingdom of Urartu and its development. The museum also houses Muslim, Byzantine, Seljuk, and Ottoman material.

150

At an altitude of 2,300 m. the spectacular ruins of the funeral monument of Antiochus I.

NEMRUD DAĞ

Nemrud Dağ is a partially isolated mountain complex situated in the northern portion of Mesopotamia. This mountain, 2150 m. high, is part of the Mount Taurus chain (*Güneydoğu Toroslar*). Its great fame in terms of monuments, which makes it an absolute must for anyone who takes a trip to Turkey, is due to the presence of one of the most extraordinary funeral monuments of antiquity, built for Antiochus I Commagene.

First mention of Commagene dates to the 8th century B.C., when it was a kingdom that was subject to the Assyrians and eventually became an Assyrian province. Subsequent unequivocable mention did not appear until 72 B.C. when it passed under the control of the Romans who allowed the prince Mithridates to style himself king. The sovereigns of Commagene were venerated as gods as were numerous Hellenistic rulers and the kings of Persia and Macedonia. This unique monumental funerary complex was built in the times of Mithridates I and his son, Antiochus I. The colossal statues, set among the divinities, were the object of worship and sacrifices. In 72 A.D., when Vespasian annexed the province of Syria, the Commagene dynasty came to an end.

The **Tumulus of Antiochus I** (1st cent. A.D.) rises up on the top of the mountain, an enigmatic complex of squared blocks of stone, greatly degraded and ruined by erosion and the frequent earthquakes. The tumulus dominates three terraced slopes on which the colossal heads and enormous slabs of stone are set. The site of the funeral shrine was apparently under this tumulus although just where the entrance was remains to be discovered.

The **East Terrace** is a sort of *pantheon* of the divinities worshipped by the Commagenes. On a podium, guarded by sculptures of an *eagle* and a *lion*, appear, one after the other, the gigantic figures of the seated gods: *Apollo-Mithra-Hermes-Helios* (assimilated into a single divinity); *Tyche* (goddess of Fortune), *Zeus Oromasdes*, Antiochus I (venerated as a god) and *Heracles-Artagnes*.

The **West Terrace** contains the same sequence of seated divinities; even though, here too, the heads of the statues have rolled to the ground, they are in a much better state of preservation than those on the eastern terrace. To be noted are the reliefs on the statue of the *Lion* which are interpreted as astronomical symbols.

The **Northern Terrace**, the most degraded, has blocks of squared stone, once part of a wall, lying here and there.

153

The Ishak Paşa Saray, the splendid castle built in 1700 in Doğubayazit.

The snow-covered peak of Mount Ararat, on which Noah's ark is said to have come to rest after the Flood.

DOĞUBAYAZIT

The city of Doğubayazit lies not far from the Iranian frontier and is a crowded stop-over along the busy international traffic routes that pass through. Considered the easternmost of the Turkish cities, it is also a good point of departure for mountain climbers who are interested in attempting to climb Mount Ararat, one of the highest mountains in the world. The surrounding landscape is dominated by the presence of an important ring of mountains all well over 3000 m. high.

The most popular tourist attraction in the immediate surroundings is the **Ishak Paşa Saray** which rises up over the valley below. This noteworthy architectural complex was built at the turn of the 17th century by Ishak Paşa, a Kurd emir on whom the sultan of Istanbul had conferred the title of governor. The imposing fortified structure controlled the old caravan routes and this permitted its owners to accumulate enormous wealth. Architecturally speaking, the building is eclectic since it is a fusion of characteristic elements of well defined styles. Of particular note are the ruins of an ancient Urartian fortification, a mosque of the Ottoman period and various rooms including the numerous harem quarters.

ARARAT

Mount Ararat, whose name goes back to the ancient Kingdom of Urartu which covered this area from the 9th century B.C. on, is known in Turkish as *Büyükağri Daği*. This giant towers up 5122 m. above sea level, casting its spell over the casual visitor and challenging the mountain climber and the trekker to dare its heights. The mountain complex with its diameter of about 40 km. is an ancient volcanic structure which rises up from the easternmost part of the Anatolian plateau. There are two main peaks, the **Great Ararat**, considered a dormant volcano, and the **Little Ararat**, thought to be spent. Between these two peaks lies the saddle known as *Sardar Bulag*. The summit is covered by perennial snows and on the northeast side there is a glacier.

Trekkers and expert mountain climbers who wish to attempt the climb up the summit must have a special visa for the mountain is situated near the frontiers of both Iran and the Soviet Union. Moreover, it would be wise to engage an expert guide due to difficulties of both a technical and environmental nature, as well as pack animals which can normally be hired at the natural points of departure such as Doğubayazit, Iğdir and Aralik.

This mountain is supposedly the biblical site where, according to the Book of Genesis, Noah's ark came to rest after the Flood. Search for the mythical ark has long stimulated the fantasy of any number of enthusiasts. After the summit was first reached at the beginning of the lst century by a French botanist, J. Pitton de Tournefort, there have been any number of attempts to find the remains of the ark cited in the Holy Scriptures and which, as evidence would have it, was hidden under the ice. Even though the catastrophical event mentioned in Genesis is accepted by official science — an event moreover which has also been assimilated into other cultures and religions, albeit with varying differences — to sustain the thesis of those who believe in the possibility of finding the mythical ark is extremely unrealistic. Even so mention must be made of presumed "sightings" reported in considerable number from the middle of the 19th century on, even though they were all accompanied by widespread skepticism on the part of the "official" scientific organs.

TRABZON

A medium-sized city overlooking the southern shores of the Black Sea, Trabzon or Trebizond is of considerable interest for the tourist, and its fortunes, past and present, are based on an intense commercial activity centered around its port.

Its origins date to the 7th century B.C. when it was founded by Miletan colonists from Sinope. Known to the ancient world as *Trapezus* either because of its ground plan or the appearance of the hills that lay behind it, the city prospered under the Romans as the capital of Pontus. Fortified by the Byzantines, it resisted all attempts at Seljuk conquest and became the seat of the Comnenes who reigned from the 13th to the 15th century. In 1461, several years after the fall of Constantinople, Trebizond too was taken over by the Ottoman Turks.

The **Fatih Camii** is situated within the originally medieval *Fortress*. This mosque is fruit of the transformation of a Byzantine basilica known as the 'Virgin of the Golden Head' (*Panaghia Chrisokephalos*) for the beauty of the gilded copper facing of the dome. Of the other mosques in the city mention should be made of the **Yeni Cuma Camii** formerly *Church of St. Eugenius*, the **Napik Camii**, once *Church of St. Andrew* (10th-11th cent.) and now in a thoroughly ruinous state, and the **Gülbahar Hatun Camii**, 16th-century structure raised near the *türbeh* (mausoleum) of the same princess. Worthy of note in the city is the ancient **Church of St. Anne** (9th cent.).

Not far from Trebizond stands the lovely basilica church of **Santa Sofia** (*Aya Sofia*), a truly fine work of architecture which was begun in the 13th century. It was transformed into a mosque at the beginning of the 17th century. Now a Museum, it contains beautiful frescoes, considered among the masterpieces of Byzantine painting (13th cent.)

Exterior of the church of Hagia Sophia in Trabzon.

The exceptional beauty of the Meryemana Manastiri in Sumela.

SUMELA

There is something unreal about the fact that monks should have lived out their tranquil lives for fifteen centuries in the midst of a landscape as harsh and wild as this, not much more than fifty kilometers from Trabzon, and more than 1200 meters above sea level. According to legend, an icon of the Virgin (painted by no less a hand than that of the apostle Luke) had come to Athens, but one day the holy image, transported by angels, crossed the ocean and landed in the grotto at the top of the Zigana mountain. Two Greek monks, Barnaba and Sophronios, who had come here to live in prayer, saw the icon and decided to dedicate a monastery to it. The fame of what was called the "Virgin of the Black Mountain" spread rapidly and increased, above all after the death of the two monks who were buried here and venerated as saints.

Probably the name *Sumela* derives from the Greek "melas" which means black and which referred not to the mountain but to the color the ancient image had undoubtedly acquired. Apparently the icon had been painted by an anonymous artist active in Trebizond in the course of the 7th (10th) century. As pilgrimages in-creased Sumela became one of the most important sites for meditation. It was in fact so important that Mohammed II, after the conquest of Trebizond in 1461, respected this holy place and conferred special protection on the monastery, later confirmed by the sultans who succeeded him. During the Greco-Turkish war however the buildings were gradually abandoned, and in 1923 the last monks left the place for good. The icon, with the authorization of the Turkish govern-ment, was taken in 1930 to the Greek monastery of Soumela, in Macedonia. The site of the monastery, with the buildings which seem to cling to the cliff that overlooks the green valley below, recalls Mount Athos and the Meteors, both in Greece.

Partially hewn out of the rock, the **Church of the As-sumption of the Virgin** was once full of frescoes, one of which commemorated the coronation of Alexis II, which took place in 1340. In the 14th century the large monastery was built against the rock wall. The first four of its five floors had 72 cells and the top floor was a gallery which also had a lookout post.

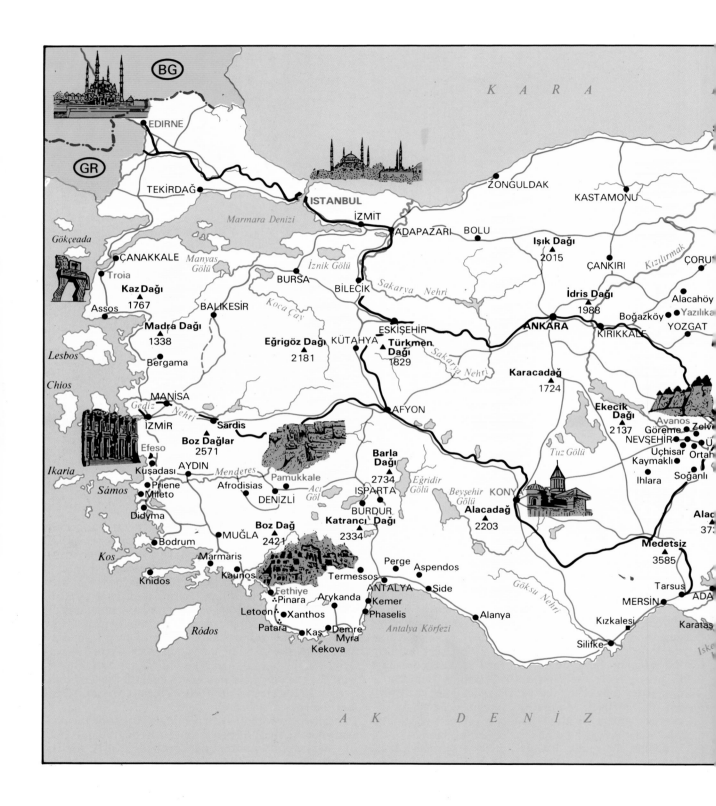

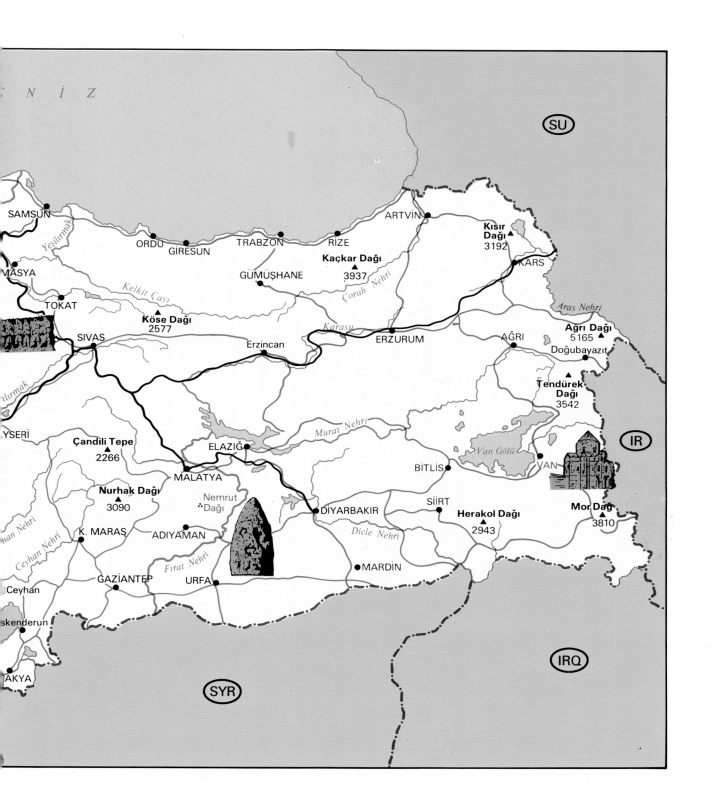

CARPET